NOV 0 4 2011

I0367281

*Praise for*

# SHUT UP AND DANCE!

"In her delicious new memoir *Shut Up and Dance!* Jamie Rose turns feminism on its head by relating how she became stronger and more secure by yielding, first on the dance floor and then in real life. Like the tango, the advice in this book is simple, elegant, brilliant, and very sexy."

—Martha Frankel, author of *Hats & Eyeglasses: A Memoir*

"A smart, funny meditation on dance, love, and one woman's path to happiness. Jamie Rose leads, inspires, and entertains—but like any good dancer, she makes it all look easy. I'm reminded of the line from *When Harry Met Sally*: 'I'll have what she's having.' In fact, I'm off to find my tango shoes right now!"

—Christina Haag, actress and *New York Times*–bestselling author of *Come to the Edge*

"There's something so wonderful about dancing with a great leader. . . . I think of myself as a strong, forward-thinking woman, but every so often it is really nice to feel taken care of."

—Samantha Harris, cohost of *Dancing with the Stars* (seasons 2–9) and correspondent and fill-in anchor of *Entertainment Tonight*

"A compulsively readable, refreshingly helpful book about how to get out of a relationship rut. Readers can start putting Rose's suggestions into practice before they even reach the final page."

—Hope Edelman, *New York Times*–bestselling author of *The Possibility of Everything* and *Motherless Daughters*

NOV 0 4 2011

# SHUT UP *and* DANCE!

THE JOY OF

LETTING GO OF THE LEAD—

ON THE DANCE FLOOR

AND OFF

# SHUT UP *and* DANCE!

# JAMIE ROSE

JEREMY P. TARCHER/PENGUIN
A MEMBER OF PENGUIN GROUP (USA) INC.
NEW YORK

**WILLARD LIBRARY, BATTLE CREEK, MI**

JEREMY P. TARCHER/PENGUIN
Published by the Penguin Group
Penguin Group (USA) Inc., 375 Hudson Street, New York, New York 10014, USA • Penguin Group
(Canada), 90 Eglinton Avenue East, Suite 700, Toronto, Ontario M4P 2Y3, Canada (a division of
Pearson Penguin Canada Inc.) • Penguin Books Ltd, 80 Strand, London WC2R 0RL, England •
Penguin Ireland, 25 St Stephen's Green, Dublin 2, Ireland (a division of Penguin Books Ltd) •
Penguin Group (Australia), 250 Camberwell Road, Camberwell, Victoria 3124, Australia (a division of
Pearson Australia Group Pty Ltd) • Penguin Books India Pvt Ltd, 11 Community Centre,
Panchsheel Park, New Delhi–110 017, India • Penguin Group (NZ), 67 Apollo Drive, Rosedale,
North Shore 0632, New Zealand (a division of Pearson New Zealand Ltd) • Penguin Books
(South Africa) (Pty) Ltd, 24 Sturdee Avenue, Rosebank, Johannesburg 2196, South Africa

Penguin Books Ltd, Registered Offices: 80 Strand, London WC2R 0RL, England

Copyright © 2011 by Jamie Rose
All rights reserved. No part of this book may be reproduced, scanned, or distributed in any
printed or electronic form without permission. Please do not participate in or encourage piracy
of copyrighted materials in violation of the author's rights. Purchase only authorized editions.
Published simultaneously in Canada

Grateful acknowledgment is made to the following for permission to reprint photos:
p. 109: *Falcon Crest* cast photo, © 1982 Gene Trindl/mptvimages.com
p. 112: Courtesy of Vladimir Estrin, www.tangoaficionado.com
p. 200: © Laura V. Mingo Photography
p. 204: Courtesy of Lee Garlington

Most Tarcher/Penguin books are available at special quantity discounts for bulk purchase for
sales promotions, premiums, fund-raising, and educational needs. Special books or book excerpts
also can be created to fit specific needs. For details, write Penguin Group (USA) Inc.
Special Markets, 375 Hudson Street, New York, NY 10014.

Library of Congress Cataloging-in-Publication Data

Rose, Jamie.
Shut up and dance!: the joy of letting go of the lead—on the dance floor and off / by Jamie Rose.
p.      cm.
ISBN 978-1-58542-889-2
1. Man-woman relationships—Psychological aspects.    2. Couples—Psychology.    3. Interpersonal
relations—Psychological aspects.    4. Ballroom dancing—Psychological aspects.    I. Title.
HQ801.R688 2011                          2011025362
646.7'7—dc23

Printed in the United States of America
1    3    5    7    9    10    8    6    4    2

BOOK DESIGN BY DEBORAH KERNER

While the author has made every effort to provide accurate telephone numbers and
Internet addresses at the time of publication, neither the publisher nor the author
assumes any responsibility for errors, or for changes that occur after publication.
Further, the publisher does not have any control over and does not assume any
responsibility for author or third-party websites or their content.

For my parents, Stewart and Reta Rose,

on or off the dance floor,

the most beautiful couple I've ever seen.

And for my beloved husband, Kip:

I would follow you anywhere.

# Contents

*Prologue*

- Are you often frustrated and angry with other people (especially your guy), thinking that it would be so much better if he or she would just do things the right way, i.e., *your* way?

- Do you ever find that the more you argue over a given point with someone (especially your man), the less you can remember what your point actually was?

- Is it sometimes difficult for you to let down your guard—to feel comfortable being soft, tender, and vulnerable?

Then you might be a woman who leads *too much*— and this book is for you.

It was a beautiful summer morning, the sun was shining, the birds were singing, and I was in the passenger seat of the car bickering with my boyfriend, a regular occurrence for us. It seemed that every time we went on a road trip we fought for at least the first half hour. What about? Oh, who knows—directions, how late we'd left, what we'd packed, anything would do.

But this day was different. I had been taking dance classes for a few months, specifically the Argentine tango—a very strict lead/follow partner dance. And suddenly the thought came to me: Why not practice some of the concepts I'd been learning in class in my relationship with my guy? Why not pretend that this conversation is a dance and let him take the lead?

Just then, my boyfriend said, angrily: "We left the house at *ten.* I wanted to leave at *nine!*"

And instead of getting defensive—countering with my usual response—something along the lines of: Well, I had a lot to *do!* And it wasn't all *my* fault! *You* were running late too! I paused, and simply said: "I know. You're right. It would have been great if we had left at nine."

He turned his head from the road to face me and opened his mouth as if to say something. But then he stopped himself and looked kind of confused. He waited for a second, and looked at me suspiciously, as if to see if I was going to add anything else, like: "But we *didn't* leave at nine, we left at ten! *Big deal!* So *what*? And it wasn't all *my* fault, blah, blah, blah . . ."

But I didn't. I kept my mouth shut, and looked right back at him, nodding my head in agreement.

Then, after a moment, his whole body relaxed. He looked back at the road and said: "Well . . . yeah, it would have been great if we'd left at nine." Then he smiled and said: "Hey, why don't you pick out a good road trip CD?"


It was transformative. When I stopped correcting, criticizing, defending, and forcing my point of view, and instead allowed him to express himself without interruption or contradiction (basically I just shut up for a minute!), he changed. Soon, what had begun as an argument turned into a conversation. We were talking and laughing and enjoying each other's company. Just how I always wanted it to be.

After this experience, I kept applying the principles and concepts I'd learned in my study of the Argentine tango—and other partner dances—to my life off the dance floor. And I found that my boyfriend and I started fighting less and had a much more harmonious relationship. While we still have our spats from time to time, I am happy to report that my guy and I now spend less time fighting and more time loving. And, we are no longer boyfriend and girlfriend, but husband and wife.

I began talking to other women I knew from the social dance scene about my discoveries and was surprised to find how many of them had had similar experiences to mine. And it wasn't just women my age. Women from ages twenty to ninety-three told me that partner dance—be it salsa, tango, swing, or country two-step—had changed their lives, and especially their relationships, for the better.

One of the major things we had all discovered is that "following" isn't what we'd thought it was; it isn't having no opinion—being a doormat. Rather, it's an equal and necessary part of being a couple—on the dance floor and off. And we don't have to always be in the role of follower just because we're women, but by *never* spending time in that role, we're missing out on a really wonderful possibility.

I realized there was a need for a book that would share the life lessons contained in the tango and other partner dances, even if you have never actually stepped onto a dance floor. (But I hope you *will*!)

This book will share what you can learn from partner dancing so you can enjoy better relationships—romantic and otherwise.

While all the lead/follow–based partner dances, like salsa, swing, ballroom, and so on, illustrate the lessons contained in this book, for the sake of clarity, I will mostly refer to the Argentine tango when I discuss *my* dancing. It's my absolute favorite dance. I love the music, the movements, and the shoes are to die for! Plus,

> "*E*verything anybody has to know about being a
> genuinely happy, attractive, loving person can be found
> at a local dance studio for the mere price of $12 a class
> ($10 if you buy the package deal)."
>
> —SAMANTHA DUNN, WRITER, SALSA DANCER

most social dancers agree that it's the hardest to learn of all the partner dances, and the most strictly lead/follow, so it provides a great way to illustrate the concepts in this book—how dancing with a partner is a metaphor for relationship.

As a result of the concepts explained in this book, I am happily married and feel more vibrantly alive and beautiful at fifty years old than I have at any other time in my life. It's my pleasure to share this essential information with other women.

Introduction

# I AM WOMAN,

---

# I AM STRONG,

---

# SO WHY AREN'T I HAPPY?

I was the go-to girl when friends needed advice. I had an opinion about everything: I could tell you what jewelry went with the dress (big earrings *or* necklace, never both); what's the best way to treat muscle strain (R.I.C.E., rest, ice, compression, elevation, and for the ice part, the best thing to use is a bag of frozen peas); how to get over a breakup (absolutely no contact—no phone calls, no e-mails, no texts, and absolutely no Facebook stalking, um, I mean, "checking"). In fact, while I was writing this paragraph, a girlfriend called to ask me about how best to treat a gynecological issue (I'm not kidding—and I'm not going into details).

This part of my personality is an asset professionally, because in addition to my acting career, I'm a teacher and director—I taught yoga for several years, am a busy acting coach, taught dramatic literature at the university level, and have directed several short films and plays. So I actually get paid for giving advice.

The problem was that I had trouble turning *off* my penchant for problem solving. My need to give my opinion sometimes trumped the fact of whether or not my listener/victim had actually *asked* for it.

M y first inkling that maybe there was something amiss came years ago when I was teaching a yoga class. I was about to give a student a correction, when suddenly the thought came to me: "Wait a minute, am I giving this person this correction because *they* need it? Or because *I* feel the need to give a correction?"

That was when I realized that perhaps this "problem solving" part of my personality had gotten out of balance. I wasn't necessarily *solving* problems, but sometimes actually *creating* them, in all my relationships, but particularly with my guy. And even though I've practiced yoga and meditation for over twenty years, and done years of therapy, it wasn't until I began learning the follower's role in the Argentine tango and other ballroom dances that my life really began to change.

## MY GUY

I had been living with my boyfriend for five years, and although I wanted to get married, he wasn't ready. His reason? We fought too much. And he was right.

Although we were madly in love with each other, we had both been married once before, and neither of us wanted to be divorced twice.

My guy is one of the funniest, smartest, and kindest people I've ever met, and it doesn't hurt that he looks like a combination of Jeff Bridges and Kevin Kline. He makes everything fun. We have an old piano in our house and in the mornings while I make our coffee, he plays show tunes and fifties' love songs and sings to me while I dance around. He's very low maintenance about food—he's sincerely grateful when I hand him a tuna sandwich for dinner (which is a very good thing, because I'm as likely to prepare a full-course home-cooked meal as Martha Stewart is to serve a frozen TV dinner at Thanksgiving).

My guy thinks I'm at my most beautiful when I'm my most natural. He doesn't give a whit about sexy lingerie and fancy hair, but likes me best in my flannel pj's and no makeup, which relieves so much pressure as I enter my sixth decade on the planet. My guy makes me laugh at least ten times every day. If I were stranded on a desert island, and I could pick only one person to be with, I'd want to be with him. But as much as I love him, he drives me absolutely crazy. And I him.

When my guy and I first met, he said of our obvious chemistry, "We're either going to fall in love and get married, or they'll find one of us on the kitchen floor with a knife in our back."

And six years into our relationship, his prophecy was beginning to feel frighteningly correct. While there was lots of love, laughs, and affection, we just couldn't seem to stop fighting.

Our fights were almost never about important issues. There were no major health or financial problems; our arguments were almost always about completely insignificant things—little power plays, like the proper position for the bathroom wastebasket, or where the heck did you put the frigging scissors?!? I'm sure you've heard the old adage to "pick your battles"? And I did. I picked all of them.

My guy is compulsively neat. But his neatness is aesthetically based, meaning, it doesn't matter where any given item is put away, just as long as it is put *away*. For example, the toilet bowl plunger can be in with the cleaning supplies (where it belongs) or it can be in the linen closet with our freshly laundered sheets and towels (which I find disgusting and slightly alarming). The stapler can be in the top left-hand drawer of my office desk, where it *belongs*, or in the bedside table in the guest room. It doesn't matter to him where a thing is, as long as it's out of sight.

I, on the other hand, am a slob, but a very organized one. My desk is a mess of old J.Crew catalogs and tattered correspondence, but if you ask me to find that letter from the Union Mission asking me if I sent in my contribution for Thanksgiving 2004, I can find it for you in ten seconds flat.

In my guy's world, when he uses an item, like the scissors—*my* office scissors—he puts them away directly after use. Where? Doesn't matter, they could be under the bathroom sink, or in the trunk of his car, as long as they're out of sight.

Me? I use the scissors, it doesn't matter that my office may look like a frat boy's dorm room after an all-night beer party, after I'm finished using them, those scissors are going directly back into the top left-hand drawer of my desk (next to the stapler). DO NOT MOVE MY SCISSORS! There isn't much I can count on in life, but when push comes to shove, I want to know that my scissors are right there in the top left-hand drawer when I need them. If I want to cut the tag off a new sweater, wrap a gift, clip an interesting article from today's newspaper, no problem, grab the scissors, snip-snip-snip, back in the drawer, done.

And what is the proper placement of the bathroom wastebasket? My guy believes it should be tucked out of sight behind the toilet. I believe it should be out in the open, ready to go. I would go into the bathroom and pull the basket out. Later, after my guy would use the facilities, I would go into the bathroom, and the basket would be pushed back in. So, I would pull the basket out, and he would go in and push the basket in, and then I would go in and pull the basket out, and then he would go in and push the basket in, and, oh, I'm getting mad just thinking about it. And he kept moving my scissors. I wanted to kill him.

Judge: Why did you violently stab your boyfriend?

Me: He moved my scissors.

Judge: Justifiable homicide. Case dismissed!

---

> *"Dancing is love's proper exercise."*
>
> —SIR JOHN DAVIES

Back in my single days I devoured every self-help book I could find on the topic of male/female relationships. And although some discussed the style differences of men and women in relationships, most of them seemed to have the primary goal of getting and keeping a man, and also advocated choosing one role, male or female—or one "energy" (I know, I know, *"energy,"* I have "New Age" leanings; I grew up in California, what can I say?)— and sticking to it for the rest of your life.

I applied some of the techniques I learned in those books to dating. For example, I stopped being "the man" when I dated, by not asking men out (more on this in Chapter Three: L is for

Listen); instead, I waited for them to call *me*. Basically I learned how to act like more of a traditional "lady" in my dating style. And I believe the new dating tools I learned from those books were instrumental in the courtship period with my husband. But once we started living together and were together 24/7, my *real* personality started coming out. I couldn't just pretend to be some sweet, meal-cooking, clothes-mending, yes-woman. I am very opinionated, ambitious, and forceful—some would say that I have a lot of archetypically masculine qualities. I could keep these qualities at bay with effort, but my "true" self always eventually reared its mustachioed head.

Now, I could work at trying to change my personality traits for the rest of my life, but I'm always going to be, let's just say, ahem, INTENSE. And my guy has a very strong personality too, so we found ourselves going head-to-head over everything, even the most mundane issues.

My guy and I loved each other, but we were like two passionate dancers doing a tango with both partners trying to lead at the same time. Instead of being sensual, flowing, and beautiful, the dance of our relationship was feeling more and more like a battle, a struggle for power.

For those of you who have not yet tried lead/follow dancing, you can think of it as being like driving a car—only one person at a time can take the wheel and steer. You can each take turns in the driver's seat, but if both of you are yanking on the wheel at the same time, chances are that car is going to crash.

I'm old enough to know that I can't change him, but I'm also old enough to know that I *can* change myself. It's like the old joke about the lightbulb and the psychiatrist. How many psychiatrists does it take to change a lightbulb? One. But the lightbulb has to *want* to change.

I wanted to change, I wanted to find a way to experience a softer, more yielding side of myself, I wanted to be able to give up the lead sometimes, to give up control, but I didn't know how.

At around the same time I was pushing for marriage with my guy, I began teaching an acting class at a local university. The focus of the classwork was for students to memorize and perform assigned material—scenes from plays and films—and then present it in class. One of my students was a professional tango dancer. When he presented his scene, he chose to improvise some moments onstage alone before his scene partner's entrance. There was no music. The stage was empty except for a small desk and couch. Slowly, the young man stood and started moving as if to music only he could hear.

His movements had a melancholy quality, a feeling of loneliness and yearning. He raised his arms as if he were embracing an invisible woman, a woman he was in love with. He took long, slow steps, extending his legs fully, and occasionally traced small circles with his feet as if he were drawing on the floor. Later I learned these movements were called lapiz, which means "pencil" in Spanish. I heard a dancer once call this "drawing your life on the floor." Watching this young man dance, I was enthralled. I somehow knew—I had an instinct—that I needed to learn this dance. That it would be the answer to something unanswered in my life. That it held a secret I needed, and wanted, to learn.

> "*We dancers are painters. We paint the music with our feet.*"
>
> —CARLOS GAVITO, WORLD-FAMOUS TANGUERO

I offered to trade private acting lessons for tango lessons. And this is where my journey began. The journey that would lead me into the relationship I wanted. The journey that would teach me the secrets of the follower: how to listen, how to wait, how to appreciate my partner, how to fully inhabit my femininity. And, perhaps most important, learn the secret of letting my guy fulfill his yearning to be my knight in shining armor, my protector, my hero, my man.

> "*I* . . . *choose a man who compels my strength, who makes enormous demands on me, who does not doubt my courage or my toughness* . . . *who has the courage to treat me like a woman.*"
>
> —ANAÏS NIN

Now, in case anyone gets the idea that I am crying out for some kind of post-feminist movement revolution, a plea to return to the sexist roles of the past, let me correct that notion right now. I am a very grateful child of the feminist movement. In the sixties, I remember not being allowed to wear pants to elementary school, and in junior high in the seventies being forced to take cooking and sewing as my "elective" courses, rather than wood and metal shop. In high school and college I joined in Women's Power marches and read Betty Friedan's *The Feminine Mystique*. I am in awe of, and forever indebted to, the fearless heroines of the feminist movement like Gloria Steinem, Shirley Chisholm, and Germaine Greer, and all the bravely subversive housewives who burned their bras and put down their frying pans. Because of their sacrifices I have seen the first female Speaker of the House, and feel certain that in my lifetime I will see the first female president of the United States.

Women are in every way as capable of leading as men, and I am so grateful to my brave sisters for paving the way so that I have a choice—I can always take the lead if I choose to. But, speaking for myself, and for many of the women (of all ages) I talked to when preparing to write this book, a result of growing up with the feeling that as a woman I needed to fight for my power was that I began to feel like I needed to *dis*-empower the men around me. It's like the swing of a pendulum, going too far in either direction: The goal is for the pendulum to find the still point—the balanced center. The proverbial battle of the sexes is still on, but as Henry Kissinger so famously said, "Nobody will ever win the battle of the sexes. There's too much fraternizing with the enemy."

According to Hanna Rosin in an article she wrote for *The Atlantic* entitled "The End of Men," collegiate women "now earn 60 percent of master's degrees, about half of all law and medical degrees . . . 42 percent of MBAs . . . and 60 percent of all bachelor's degrees." In the coming decade, women will be overtaking men in the workforce. So, is this truly the "end of men"? I hope not, I love men and want to keep them around. I know that my man needs to feel important and needed. I don't need to diminish myself to make this happen, but I do need to empower him, I need to make him feel needed. Why? Not because of any political agenda but because of a romantic one. When he feels needed and important, he's more loving, and a better partner, and when I allow him to partner with me, I feel connection—union—I feel loved.

When preparing to write this book I had a discussion with prominent Los Angeles psychiatrist Philip Stutz, M.D. He told me that in Jungian analytical psychology there is the concept of male and female archetypes, the *animus* (male) and the *anima* (female), and that the inner personalities of both men and women contain both archetypes. He said that what happened after the feminist revolution was that some women got the idea that they had to behave like men to have power. Which is actually, in a way, making the statement that women are inferior to men. In our conversation Dr. Stutz said, "If you think that you need to act like a man—archetypically speaking—to have power, then paradoxically you are actually saying that to you the female archetype is not powerful . . . The 'follower's' role (in partner dancing) is a living embodiment of a female power . . . self-identification as a female that is not trying to ape the man—not trying to be like the man at all, but is still very powerful in its own right. You don't have to enter the maleness of things in order to have power."

In this book, when I talk about the roles of the "woman" and the "man," and use terms like "femininity" and "masculinity," and the "follower" and the "leader," I'm talking about archetypes, about energetic qualities. I am not being literal. You can be a man and explore the role of follower and be a woman and explore the role of leader. They are not necessarily gender-specific. And you don't need to choose one role for the rest of your life. But in a relationship, just as in ballroom dancing, if two people are both trying to lead at the same time, the dance falls apart.

In Argentine tango, as in other partner dances, the leader's role is to suggest a move, and the follower's role is to execute the move beautifully, interjecting her personal interpretation in a way that doesn't conflict with the basic structure created by the leader, but enhances it. It's as if the leader is the architect, and the follower is the interior designer. You need both to make a beautiful environment—structure without embellishment is cold and dull, while decoration without form can be cluttered and superficial.

Close your eyes for a moment and picture the archetypal image of a tango couple. Notice the man: Does he not have some traditionally "feminine" qualities? The elegant fluidity of his movement, the refined and dapper suit, the deliberately groomed hair, the pointed toes? Now, notice the woman. Does she not have some traditionally "masculine" qualities? A kind of fierceness and strength? Is she wearing stiletto heels? Like *knives* on her feet? In Argentina, where the tango was born, they don't even use the terms "lead" and "follow," but rather, "man" and "woman." The dance is a relationship; its goal is union, both spiritual and physical. Union not of two opposites, where one partner dominates and the other obeys, but of two equals, with separate but complementary qualities. Like any good relationship, it is an exchange of energies—an intimate and loving conversation.

# A SHORT GLOSSARY OF TERMS

When I discuss the Argentine tango, I will occasionally use certain Spanish words to describe aspects of the dance. I'll use these terms sparingly, and will always offer a brief explanation when I use them in the text of the book. But here is a short list:

*Boleo:* a tango embellishment that involves a quick sweeping move of the leg. The movement can be high off the ground or low. The leg moves like the lashing of a whip.

*Gancho:* a move in which a partner hooks his or her leg under or around some part of his or her partner's body.

*Giros:* a word that means "turns" in Spanish. Where a tango couple spins around each other while maintaining an embrace.

*Lapiz:* a move in which the dancer caresses the floor with the edge of his or her foot or toe, making circular designs.

*Milonga:* a place where people go to dance tango. (Note: In addition to being a location, a "milonga" is also a playful rhythmic style of tango music and dance. I know, confusing, but in this book I will only use the word milonga to refer to a place where people dance the tango.)

*Ochos:* "eights" in Spanish. This is a basic tango move in which partners move backward or forward, turning their hips while they walk, so they literally move in figure eights across the floor.

*Tanda:* a set of three to five tango songs.

*Tanguera:* a female tango dancer.

*Tanguero:* a male tango dancer.

# I WILL NOT FOLLOW YOU!
# ANYWHERE!

My biggest challenge when learning the tango and other partner dances was not the physical movement but the concept of *following*. I had no problem taking center stage, delegating, instructing, analyzing problems and solving them, but I had very little experience in the softer, more archetypically feminine concepts of yielding, waiting, allowing, receiving, listening, and supporting.

Before I took up ballroom dancing, I always felt as though for anything to work out I had to be the actor *and* the director. It was as if I thought I had to be the chair of the committee and the committee too. It wasn't until I started dancing with a partner that I discovered that "following" wasn't what I thought it was. It didn't mean having no opinion, being a doormat, or some kind of yes-dear-whatever-you-say-dear type woman. It was quite another thing. A new possibility. It allowed me the space to just listen and interpret, to simply enjoy, rather than always having to be the one deciding everything. And you know what? It was kind of nice.

I've always been terrible at sports—as a child I was always the last one picked for the team. Yes, I was *that* kid. Flaming red curly hair and braces on my teeth, complete with protruding metal neck gear. I was the prime target in all the dodge ball games. And as a result, I was chronically afraid of any sport involving a ball. I have very strong memories of staring at my feet while the team captains made their choices. *No one* wanted me on their team. So I had no concept of what it meant to be a "team player." And ballroom dancing is most definitely a team sport.

At the age of forty-five, learning to follow, to be part of a team, felt not only awkward, but impossible. My first attempts were clumsy. But whenever I felt frustrated, I remembered the beautiful image of that student dancing alone and the strong feeling it had evoked in me. And although I still didn't really understand why, my intuition kept telling me to keep at it. And I did.

The dance floor became a kind of laboratory to experiment with the softer aspects of myself in relationship with another person, a place where I could let my guard down. It was too hard to work on it with my guy, there was too much water under that bridge, too many old resentments, and habitual ways of relating. And honestly, I was too prideful at first to work on it at home: I had a big investment in being right—as opposed to being happy. But in dance class, with strangers, there was no history, no need for relationship power plays. Dancing offered me a way to literally step into the follower's role for a change, to try it on in a safe, nonpolitical atmosphere, a place to even sometimes (egads!) let my partner take the lead.

When dancing with my partners, I practiced keeping my mouth shut. If a step wasn't working out, I didn't offer opinions on how to fix things, rather, I patiently supported my partner while he figured it out. I just made it my business to pay attention—to try to follow whatever he was trying to lead me through. If he asked me how it felt—if he was holding me in an uncomfortable way or rushing me through the moves—I would answer honestly, but I didn't correct him, or tell him he was doing it wrong.

> "*I can always spot women who really don't want to allow the men to lead. I see it in their bodies, in the way that they move. They are like rocks—you can't get their arms to bend or their joints to move.*"
>
> —LAURA CANELLIAS,
> PROFESSIONAL SALSA DANCER AND TEACHER

A few months after I started dancing tango I was practicing with one of my regular partners and I could tell he was frustrated. When I asked him what was wrong he said: "I just feel that you're fighting the lead."

I asked him what that meant. And he said: "Well, it's like every time I suggest a move, your body says no."

I felt as if I just had cold water splashed in my face. This was almost exactly like something my boyfriend had been telling me was driving him crazy about my behavior in our relationship.

One of my guy's major complaints was that whenever he made a request of me, whether it was to try a new restaurant, or run an errand, like stopping at the dry cleaner's for him on my way home, my first response was always "No."

I always had some excuse, like, "I'm on a diet." Or "I don't have time." But, my first response, justified or not, was always to resist.

Sometimes, after initially rejecting one of my guy's suggestions, a moment later I would try to backtrack, saying something like: "Actually, now that I think about it, trying a new restaurant sounds like fun" or "Sure, no problem picking up your dry cleaning, it's right on my way." But it would be too late. The damage had been done. Often, he'd put a lot of time into finding a new fun thing for us to do together and had been excited about sharing it with me and I shot him down. Again and again.

Why? At the time I didn't know. But now I realize it was fear. I was afraid of spontaneity, of giving up control. Why? Because if I gave up control, I was vulnerable; and that scared me. What if my partner led me right off a cliff?

If I'm going to follow someone else's lead, I need to know that he's worthy of following, that he cares about my well-being, that he cares about my wishes. It is foolish and potentially dangerous to just blindly follow any leader. (More on how to identify a good leader later in this book.) But when I really got honest with myself, I had to admit that I was resistant to all leads. Good and bad. Actually, it was lack of control that I was most afraid of.

OK, at this point I need to tell you a bit about my painful childhood. I know, I know, you've heard it before and probably much worse and of course have your own problems, but I need to share a bit about how I became such a controlling nut job (I mean, woman with, um, let's just say, *control issues*). You guessed it! It's all my mother's fault! (Sorry, Mom.)

# MOMMY DEAREST

My parents were both in show business. Mom was a Radio City Music Hall Rockette and danced at the famous New York nightclub the Latin Quarter (Barbara Walters's father, Lou Walters, owned the club).

Dad was a singer; he played the lead roles in a lot of famous musicals like *Oklahoma!* and *Guy and Dolls* on the summer stock circuit (the term "summer stock" refers to touring productions of major Broadway musicals and plays performed in the summer months. It was very popular in the fifties and sixties). My parents actually *met* in a show. Dad saw this gorgeous, long-legged redhead in the chorus line and it was love at first sight. When they got married, Mom was nineteen and Dad was twenty-five.

Mom gave up her dance career when my brother and I were little and my dad traveled around the country doing summer stock and performing in nightclubs. Money was tight in our family—we had enough for a nice home but both my parents had to work hard to afford it and there wasn't any money left over. Dad traveled constantly for work and was rarely home (our family joke was that we called him "Uncle Daddy"), so for several years Mom basically raised my brother and me on her own. Caught between the paradigm of the fifties housewife and the then-new image of the seventies-style working woman, Mom worked full-time as a real estate agent and yet still did her best to have dinner on the table for us every night. No one was waiting with milk and cookies

*My parents, Reta and Stewart Rose, in costume, backstage.*

*Reta and Stewart Rose on their wedding day.*

when my brother and I came home from school; we would while away the hours (my brother doing homework, me watching TV or talking to my friends on the phone) until Mom finally got home from work at six or seven—stressed out and exhausted. Then, after a long day at the office she'd frantically whip dinner together while fielding calls from nervous clients. Sometimes, shortly after arriving home, she would suddenly have to rush out again to present an offer or show a house, once more leaving us alone.

There is one image of that time that is indelibly burned into my memory. I was in sixth grade. It was a school night. It was very late, maybe eleven o'clock, and I was in bed, but too excited to sleep. The next day there was to be a special graduation ceremony to celebrate my class's passage from elementary school to junior high. As I lay there tossing and turning, I heard a whirring sound. I got out of bed and stuck my head out into the dark hallway to investigate and realized it was the sound of my mother's sewing machine.

I snuck quietly down the hall and sat on the floor in the doorway of her sewing room and watched her as she worked. The only light in the dark room came from the sewing machine itself, and it illuminated her face as she ran some kind of gauzy material under the up and down of the needle, furrowing her brow as she scrutinized its passage through the machine. She was making me a dress for the ceremony. I'll never forget her face—drawn, exhausted, but so concentrated and intent, and her pale hands pushing and pulling the fabric—white dotted swiss—as she worked, alone, late into the night.

Now that I'm an adult and look back, I have such compassion

for my mother's sacrifices; she tried to become some kind of a superwoman—both mother and father to my brother and me. It was as if she felt that if she could only do enough—sell enough houses, cook enough dinners, sew enough dresses—that our family would be OK, that she could somehow control the outcome of our lives just as she controlled the fabric of my dress in her sewing machine. And I was her apt pupil.

With my mom as my example, I grew up feeling that as a woman I needed to do everything on my own—I needed to be all things to all people and I couldn't expect any help. And while I admired (and still do) her independence and take-charge, can-do personality, and am grateful for her stellar influence (without her example I wouldn't have accomplished half of what I have in my life, including writing this book), I recognized the loneliness in that image of her working at her sewing machine late into that night.

And the wonderful fact is that our family did turn out OK. But we didn't make it through the hard times because of the dinners, or the money, or the dresses, but because of the love. Shortly after that time, when my mom was working herself to death trying to keep everything going on her own, my father woke up to the fact that my mom deserved and needed a real partner. He changed jobs and we all moved to a new city so that he and my mom could raise our family together. And to this day, the closeness of my family is one of the great blessings of my life.

# JUST SAY YES!

So when my partner told me I was "fighting the lead," I recognized it as an opportunity—a chance to learn how to step out of the stressful and often lonely position of feeling like I was on my own, that I needed to always be in control. And by that time it was clear to me that if I wanted a happier relationship with my guy, I had to learn how to back off sometimes and let him take charge. And he, of course, was not only fully capable of it, he liked the feeling—it made him feel honored, respected, and, well, like a man.

I made a decision to do an experiment. I put myself on a "just say yes" diet and silently promised myself that I would say yes to whatever my guy asked me to do for twenty-four hours.

Now, if my guy was abusive in some way, or had some kind of weird sexual fantasies, this would be a bad idea. But my guy's worst quality is just that he's, well, let's just call it *frugal.* When it comes to entertainment planning he's up for anything, as long as it's free. Luckily we live in Los Angeles so there are a lot of really great free cultural activities readily available, but occasionally he does kind of miss the mark. Like the time he got us free tickets for the mariachi *vs.* klezmer "battle of the bands." Or the experimental mime version of *The Trojan Women* at the Getty Museum. So while his suggestions are sometimes boring or annoying, they're not dangerous. (Although the mariachi–klezmer fracas may have resulted in a few torn ligaments among the more zealous participants.)

So on the day when I decided to do my "exercise in affirming," my guy approached me and said, "What are your plans tomorrow?"

I hated when he asked general questions like that. He didn't say why he was asking—what I might be signing myself up for if I told him I was free. It could be a mariachi *vs.* klezmer band rematch, for God's sake! But I reminded myself of my inner promise to say yes no matter what, and said, smiling through my fear: "Um. Tomorrow's flexible. What do you have in mind?"

He said, "You'll probably say no, but I just got some free tickets to the Red Sox game. They're in town playing the Dodgers."

Now, there is very little I detest in life as much as watching baseball. I come from a family of baseball fanatics. When we were little, my dad used to bring my brother and me to all the LA Dodgers games and we would always sit in the bleachers. And do you know why they call them the bleachers? BECAUSE THE SUN IS SO STRONG THERE IT BLEACHES THE SEATS! And may I remind you that I am a natural redhead? And this was the 1960s, *before* everyone had realized the importance of sunblock! To me, baseball conjures up images of red, blistered, peeling skin—my little body slathered in gloppy white peaks of menthol-scented Noxzema skin cream. To this day I am constantly in the dermatologist's office having bits of my body scraped off due to those years of baking in the bleachers.

But I had made a commitment, so I said with as much enthusiasm as I could muster, "Um, sure!"

And prayed that it was a night game.

My guy looked shocked.

"Really?" he said.

"Sure. Peanuts and Cracker Jack! Woo! Sounds great . . . um . . . when?"

He grinned. And he looked so happy that I thought to myself, "Why the heck did I wait so long to do this? So, big deal, I may have to sit in the bleachers, what's another basal-cell carcinoma? And anyway, that's why God created SPF 70. And hats. And hazmat suits."

And then my guy said: "Tomorrow night."

"A night game," I thought to myself. "Thank God." And you know what? I had a great time.

> "*All you need is love, love is all you need.*"
>
> —THE BEATLES

That experience with my guy, as well as many others I will relate later in this book, showed me that through my study of the tango I'd stumbled (quite literally sometimes—just ask some of my early dance partners!) onto insights that could be helpful to others. As I noticed the way the skills I was learning in dance class were trickling out to the rest of my life, I began to realize that the Argentine tango and other partner dances had a lot more to offer than just having a good time on the dance floor. Dancing was showing me how to be a better friend, a better partner in my relationships—it was showing me how to *love*.

I started sharing my discoveries with other women, those who danced as well as those who didn't. And I found that many of them related and were hungry for the relationship tools I was learning in dance class. As I looked more closely, I realized that the basis of all the lessons I was learning was really *love*. And the concepts could actually be broken down into elements using the letters of that word: L.O.V.E.

Listen, Open Your Heart, Voice Your Desires, and Embrace.

In this book I will share through anecdotal experiences—my own and others—how you can use the principles of L.O.V.E. to improve your relationships, whether or not you ever step onto a dance floor.

But before you're ready to L.O.V.E., you need to be fully committed to a loving relationship with yourself. That's why the next chapter is called:

Your First Partner Is You.

*chapter one*

# YOUR FIRST PARTNER IS *You*

*"When you're dancing, you don't dance to every part of the music, sometimes you pause. And it's in the pauses that you discover your own music."*

—PABLO VILLARRAZA,
PROFESSIONAL TANGUERO AND
CO-FOUNDER, DNI TANGO, BUENOS AIRES

Most psychologists and relationship experts agree that to truly love another person, you must love yourself first. Likewise, before you're ready to practice the principles of L.O.V.E., you need to be able to feel whole and balanced dancing alone—you have to become your own first partner.

> *"If you feel incomplete, you alone must fill yourself with love in all your empty, shattered spaces."*
>
> —OPRAH WINFREY

In tango dancing sometimes the footwork is so quick and subtle that the only two people completely aware of the movements are the two dancers performing them. In order to allow for this kind of intricate improvisation, it's essential that both dancers always maintain their own center of balance. This is called maintaining your own *axis*. Think of it as being like how the earth rotates around its own axis. While it spins, it is virtually wrapping around itself. So you are in fact spinning around yourself—your own center—while you're dancing with another person. Otherwise you would be depending on *them* as your center of gravity.

Because of my many years of yoga practice and my childhood dance training, I'm very flexible and kinesthetically aware, so I was able to do a lot of the fancier tango embellishments early on in my dancing. I could kick my leg up high in my boleos and perform beautiful lapiz but often I would have to push down on my partners for balance. I was overly dependent on them. If they were to walk away suddenly I would fall right over.

In dance, as in any good relationship, you do, of course, sometimes rely on your partner to hold you up—good friends provide a shoulder to cry on when the chips are down, and married life rarely works out so that both partners are evenly giving fifty/fifty. In fact, I once heard someone say that in a good marriage both partners need to give 100 percent. And there are some tango moves where you literally lean your whole body weight into your partner, but even in this case, you need to have your wits about you, or you'll go crashing down to the floor if your partner loses his footing. You have to be able to find the balance between standing strong and letting go. You never want to hang on to your partner for dear life like a drowning man pulling his rescuer under the waves. No one, leader or follower, wants to feel like they are carrying around a dead weight.

The art of embellishments in tango is that you should be able to do them without disrupting the balance of your partner, or your own balance. This goes for both men and women, for lead and follow. I hate it when a leader is trying to show off some fancy dance moves beyond his skill level. I've had two-hundred-pound men literally lean their weight on me, requiring me to hold them up while they lamely execute some fancy move they saw on *Dancing With the Stars*. I've experienced bruised shins and smashed toenails dancing with guys like this. After dancing with them, I feel beat up and exhausted. And likewise I shouldn't require my leader to support my weight and to hold my balance for me when we're dancing as if I were recovering from knee surgery and he were a metal walker.

You may be seeing the metaphor here. In a romantic relationship, or even a platonic friendship, I need to be grounded—I need to be able to carry my own weight. I need to feel complete on my own before I am really qualified to share my life with another person. Like most things in life, I learned this lesson the hard way.

> "*You marry to the level of your self-esteem.*"
>
> —MARIE OSMOND

At age twenty-six I had what I like to call a "practice" marriage. The wedding was a big fat fancy affair at the famous Los Angeles landmark the Hotel Bel-Air. The day was replete with sumptuous floral displays, a harpist, celebrity guests, and even a man-made creek on which floated a pair of live swans, which leisurely swam by from time to time, as if on cue, setting the stage for romantic perfection.

My fiancé, dashing and handsome in black tie and tails, was a successful screenwriter, and I, dripping in ecru lace and seed pearls, had just finished starring as the lead in a TV series called

*Lady Blue*. We were the perfect Hollywood couple, having the perfect Hollywood wedding. The only problem was, I wasn't in love with the groom. I mean, I really, really liked him—A LOT! I appreciated him—he was handsome, and smart, and funny, and successful. Any woman would have been thrilled to marry him! But, well, I just didn't have those little flutters I always thought I would have when marrying the love of my life.

During the months of our engagement I tried to convince myself I was in love with him—I mean, he was perfect—so there must have been something wrong with *me*. I thought, well, maybe this is what marriage-love feels like—no flutters, just deep appreciation, a kind of strong friendship, like back in the days of arranged marriage. Like in India. Or in *Fiddler on the Roof.* I would *learn* to love him. Yes! I would!

Finally, our wedding day came, the happiest (supposedly) day of my life. It was a perfect early summer day. (Yes, I was even a June bride.) And I stood with my father, waiting for our cue to walk down the aisle. I looked down the line of smiling guests to the spot where my betrothed stood waiting with the man who would be performing our wedding—a California supreme court judge. In retrospect, I realize that perhaps our choice of marriage officiators should have been a bit of a red flag. I mean, the guy was qualified to impose the death penalty. But there I stood, arm in arm with my dad, a huge fake smile plastered on my face, ready to take the walk that now was beginning to feel a bit like "the green mile" of Stephen King fame, when I heard Wagner's "Here Comes the Bride"—dum dum da dum, dum dum da dum—and I froze. I turned to my father and said, "Daddy, am I making a mistake?"

And I knew I was. My dad looked confused—should he run

me out of there or was this just cold feet? But I thought about how everyone was there waiting and smiling and how we'd already paid (a fortune) for everything—the flowers, the dress, the harp, the swans—and suddenly, my actor's "The show must go on" gene kicked in. I smiled at my worried dad, nodded that I was ready (he looked extremely relieved), and down the aisle I went.

Afterward we had a fabulous reception—a live band, lots of dancing. We had an absolutely gorgeous wedding. But no marriage took place that day. Our union lasted exactly one year.

## LOVE JUNKIE

After my first marriage I spent about ten years getting my heart broken, over and over again. I kept trying to fit myself into relationships with guys whose relationship styles and personalities didn't suit mine, because I desperately wanted to be part of a couple.

During those years, I had a two-year relationship in which I was almost addicted to my partner. The relationship was extremely romantic, and completely unhealthy. We were obsessed with each other. We were like a couple of junkies, and our drug of choice was love. Our love affair provided the kind of highs described in the greatest romantic literature—it was as fierce and tortured as Cathy and Heathcliff's of *Wuthering Heights*, and as tender and intensely poetic as Romeo and Juliet's (or so we believed). The only problem was, all of these famous star-crossed lovers *died* at the end of their stories. In the real world, this kind of romantic love has a very short shelf life.

We were together constantly. We spent hours reading poetry

to each other in bed. We especially loved the suicidal poets: lots of Anne Sexton and Sylvia Plath. And we went on fantastic trips to romantic destinations like Costa Rica and Paris. But our relationship wasn't "other" friendly. We didn't go to parties, we never got together with friends. We lived in a kind of cocoon of romantic intoxication. But it turned out that our love was an illusion— like a mirage that turns to dry sand when you look too closely. And while our relationship was very passionate and very exciting, it was also very painful.

I gave up my whole life to be with this man. He was a successful artist and traveled a lot to show his work, and I went with him. I was out of town during very busy times in my career. My agents constantly called, asking me when I would again be available for work. But I was always too busy with my boyfriend. I missed an entire year of auditions at a critical time in my career. My agents dropped me. I lost friends due to neglect. Then, my boyfriend started getting very jealous. He accused me all the time of flirting with other guys (the fact that I was never out of his sight long enough to *see* other guys never seemed to occur to him). I stopped wearing makeup and getting my hair styled. I dressed "down" in a way that hid my body. I tried everything to make myself as small as possible in the hopes of somehow making him comfortable.

At one point, he asked me to move in with him. I agreed happily, but since my condo was only a few blocks from his place, to avoid the cost of hiring movers (since I had stopped working I didn't have much money), I did the move slowly, just a few pieces of furniture and boxes at a time. My boyfriend accused me of taking too much time bringing over my things because I didn't really want to move in—it was proof that I didn't really love him. Finally, I hired a truck and a moving crew. And once my things were in the house, he complained that I was *un*packing too slowly. So I hurried to unpack and within a week or so had everything set up just right—my office was in order, all of my clothes were put away, my knickknacks were displayed just the way I like them—the place felt like home.

The night I finally finished, I put all of the cardboard boxes out to be recycled and crawled into bed next to my boyfriend, feeling happy and excited to start this new phase of our life together. The next day he broke up with me. He told me he felt I was "crowding" him.

I was destroyed. I had built my whole life around him. I had completely abandoned myself for his love. I was sick with grief. Getting over the breakup took months; I couldn't sleep, lost fifteen pounds that I couldn't afford to lose, I couldn't work. I was like a junkie detoxing from heroin. And when I finally got over him, I vowed never—*never* to let that happen again.

## I COULD LIVE IN A YURT (BUT I DON'T REALLY WANT TO)

But in the subsequent years, I still made mistakes, I still had further to go before I "hit bottom" as they say, and really learned how to be my own best partner. I still kept trying to change who I was in order to make things work with whatever guy I was currently attracted to.

I remember at one point, frustrated at my tendency to forget myself and my needs as soon as I felt romantic chemistry with a man, I actually made a list of the qualities I wanted in a mate. A kind of wish list. Ideally, I wanted a man who was between thirty-five and forty-five, was fully established in his career (he didn't have to be rich—just not struggling), and definitely wanted kids. It would also be wonderful if he happened to own his own home (I'd been living in an apartment since that last big breakup with Romeo/Heathcliff, and really missed living in a house). In my fantasies, I would love a fireplace, a yard, and enough rooms that my man and I could each have our own space. Again, this wasn't a deal-breaker, but it was on my wish list.

Soon after making my list, I met a handsome yoga teacher. He was built like a Greek god, had long flowing black hair, the most beautiful blue eyes I'd ever seen on a man, and his well-muscled arms were festooned with colorful tattoos depicting images from the *Bhagavad Gita*. One day he invited me to join him for tea after his class. Over chai lattes with soy milk we began to tell each other our life stories. He was forty-eight. I thought of my wish list: "Well," I thought, "he's close enough to my age range, let's not split hairs." Check!

Then he told me that he had tried his hand at several careers: musician, actor, car salesman, but none of them had worked out. He had recently declared bankruptcy (for the second time) and just become a full-time yoga teacher two months ago.

I went back to my list, "Um, well, maybe being established in his career isn't that important—money isn't everything—how shallow of me—he's happy!" OK, check!

Then he shared his belief that the world was vastly overpopulated, and so he had recently undergone a vasectomy.

"Oh no," I thought, "I want kids! . . . but you know, he is SO CUTE! Those eyes . . . maybe we could adopt!" So I asked, trying to sound casual of course, "Oh, I do see your point about over-population, there sure are a lot of parentless kids in the world. Would you ever consider adoption?"

"No," he replied, "I don't see myself ever becoming a father, I love my independence too much. I need my freedom. I'd like to make a pilgrimage to India at some point, maybe spend a year or so studying with my guru, it's just too complicated with kids."

"Oh yeah, I can see that," I said, thinking, "hmmm . . . perhaps in a few years he'll change his mind . . . yes! I'm sure I'll be able to convince him to adopt! Maybe a poor Indian child!" Check!

We sipped our lattes and I asked him where he lived. He told me that he had just moved into a yurt in Ojai.

"A yurt? What's a yurt?" I asked.

"It's like a big round tent," he replied, "with a wood floor. There's no electricity or running water, but I don't mind. I love the idea of simplifying my life."

"Oh," I said, looking into his beautiful, black-lashed, tropical beach-blue eyes, and I thought to myself, "I could live in a yurt."

> *"Do you want to meet the love of your life? Look in the mirror."*
>
> —BYRON KATIE

At this point, thanks to the intervention of a few loving girlfriends, I finally woke up. I realized that if I had any degree of sexual chemistry with a guy it was like I became hypnotized and was an absolute pushover. If I was going to save my-self from ever having to again endure a kind of death-by-romance relationship, I needed to learn how to be in a relationship with myself. So I put myself on a romance diet. I became my own boyfriend. Really. I began dating myself. And I turned out to be the best boyfriend I'd ever had!

I'd take myself out to nice restaurants (since I have always loved reading, a book would supply the exciting dinner conversation); I went to movies, concerts, and plays by myself (a habit I still enjoy because it's much easier to get a great seat at a hot concert or theatrical event if you are buying just one ticket); I bought myself little gifts from time to time and the presents were always perfect! Exactly what I wanted!

I spent more than a few New Year's Eves alone in my apartment watching Dick Clark rock in the New Year on TV and kissing the cat at midnight. And it wasn't even my cat. I had to borrow my neighbor's. I went on little trips by myself. I went to Big Bear and took skiing lessons, I went to the Kern River and joined a group kayaking trip. One really great thing about traveling alone is that as the odd man (or woman) out, you often get special treatment. For example, on the river trip, all the two-person kayaks were taken by couples and/or friends traveling together. But as a sin-gle, I got to go with the guide. And he was a *fireman*—a hand-some, blond, thirty-five-year-old FIREMAN! (I'm just saying.)

After my "romance diet" I had proved to myself I could live (and live well) without a man. And I was very happy with my independent lifestyle. But, while I was no longer desperate for a relationship, I was lonely. I didn't necessarily want to live in a yurt, but I didn't want to have to live alone for the rest of my life with a borrowed cat either. And that's when I met my guy.

A friend of mine offered to set me up on a blind date with a friend of his. I thought, "Blind date? No way." Then the friend told me that the guy he wanted to set me up with was extremely handsome, funny, and successful. "Hmmm," I thought, "he doesn't sound like my usual type—sullen, emotionally unavailable, and broke, I don't know," but then I remembered that continually dating my "type" had gotten me where I was—thirty-six, single, and not only childless, I didn't even own a plant—so I thought perhaps I should give this guy a try.

We met for breakfast (much less pressure than a dinner date, and, of course, cheaper) and our meal lasted well into lunch. For our second date he invited me to the racetrack. He told me to "dress appropriately." When he came to pick me up at my apartment I opened the door wearing my wedding dress. (Hey! I spent a lot of money on that dress—I wanted a second wearing!) He looked kind of shocked—his eyes grew wide and he kind of pulled back a little—but then he burst out laughing. And that's when I fell in love with him.

Still, we took it slow. Both of us had already been married once before, so we wanted to make sure it was right before we made that kind of commitment again. We dated for three years before we decided to move in together.

Things went well for the first few years, but then I became frustrated that our relationship wasn't moving forward. I was feeling ready to make a deeper commitment—to get married—but my guy wasn't. I was convinced that the problem was his lack of commitment. But at one point I started wondering if perhaps I was the one with the coldest feet.

The house I share with my guy has three levels; the top floor is an open loft, and this is the area my guy chose as his office space. There are no doors or walls in his office. He is always available.

For my office, I chose the smallest room at the end of a long hall on the bottom floor—as far away from my guy's office as possible. I always kept my office door closed. And outside on the doorknob I placed one of those DO NOT DISTURB signs they have in hotels.

I was so fiercely determined not to lose my autonomy, to never again be a doormat, that I was pushing my guy away. The boundaries I had learned in my single years had become walls. I was like a person who had a problem driving their car off the road to the right; the answer is not to drive the car off the road to the left, but to learn how to drive down the middle of the road. I needed to learn how to be secure in myself, but not in a rigid, unmovable way. I wanted to be independent, but not so much so that I might as well have been living alone. It was like I was afraid that if I let down my guard, I would revert back to the girl I was before, the one who had her heart broken so many times. I was holding a big part of myself back. Because I was afraid. I was saying I wanted marriage—a deeper commitment. But I had that DO NOT DISTURB sign on my door. And as the saying goes, actions speak louder than words.

# FROM DOORMAT TO GODDESS

A few months into my tango dancing, I was at a phase where I was really struggling. I had gotten feedback from some of the men I danced with that they felt like I wasn't moving dynamically, that there was a tentative quality to my steps. I listened to their feedback but it didn't really strike home with me until I saw a videotape of myself dancing with one of my regular partners. When I looked at the tape, I was shocked. I didn't look at all like I imagined. Instead I looked timid, unsure, weak! It didn't make sense. I'd been a professional actress since I was a child and I was very comfortable in the spotlight; in fact, at age six my dancing got me my very first acting job (go-go dancing with Bugs Bunny in a Kool-Aid commercial). While not a professional dancer, I had always had a lot of natural aptitude and had always felt great moving to music. But with my partner, I looked terrible! I danced as if I had no opinion—like a scared little girl. No wonder I didn't want to let a man lead me! Being led transformed me from a strong, in-control woman into a frightened, tentative child.

That video of me dancing made me realize that in many ways I had developed a kind of false confidence—it only worked if I was in control of a situation—if I danced alone. When I danced with a partner, I flipped between resisting the lead or following along like a docile child.

I wondered if it was possible for me to retain my confidence if I wasn't playing choreographer? Or was it either/or for me? Was my choice either to dance alone or lead? Or, was it possible for me to find a way to be so authentically confident, so self-possessed that I didn't disappear as soon as I let a man lead me?

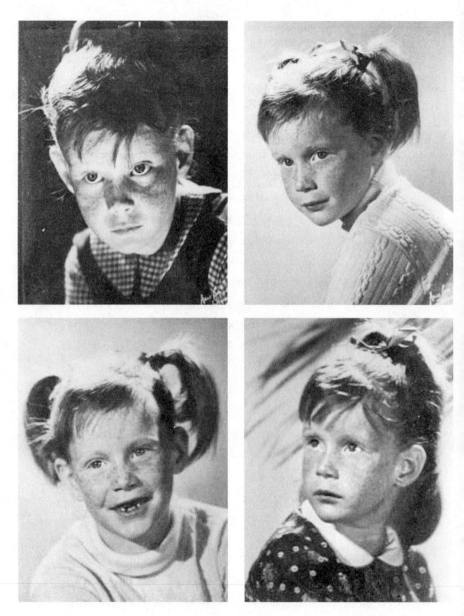

*My first professional acting pictures, age six.*

In order for me to feel safe letting another person have a voice, to take the lead sometimes, I needed to feel fully secure and powerful within myself. I thought I had already learned this lesson, but the dance floor showed me that I had much more to learn.

In life, if my happiness is conditional upon outside events, I'm in big trouble. If I want to be happy, I have to be able to deal with whatever life gives me. I can't shrink or fall apart if things don't go my way or where I expected them to go. And I also can't push life away by trying to control everyone and everything.

I wanted to feel whole and balanced in any situation—in dance and in life. I wanted *unconditional* confidence. And to do that, I needed to find my inner goddess.

*chapter two*

# YOUR INNER *Goddess*

*"The goddess was discovered by her gait."*

—VIRGIL

G oddess"—such a powerful and evocative word. For me it conjures images of Isis with her ankh and staff, Diana with her quiver of arrows, and Venus emerging from the ocean froth in her half-shell. In my Webster's dictionary, a goddess is defined as "a woman whose great charm or beauty arouses adoration."

Now, not all of us are born beautiful—Julia Roberts? Halle Berry? Sophia Loren? Come on—these ladies were gorgeous from birth. And even if we're lucky enough to be born with physical beauty—I don't care how many expensive creams you use or knives you go under—it fades. It's just a plain fact of life.

## DO YOU BELIEVE IN MAGIC?

So if beauty fades, how do we retain our goddess natures and continue to receive the adoration we deserve? Referring back to the definition in my trusty Webster's, a goddess is adored not only for her beauty, but also for her *charm*. And charm is defined as "a trait that fascinates, allures or delights . . . as if by magic."

Now, we can't all necessarily control the fact of whether or not we are physically beautiful, but my contention is that we all have the ability to be charming, alluring, and delightful—to make magic. Charm is a way of being in the world. It's how we live our lives. It's a decision, not something that just happens to us out of the blue. And we have to set the stage for magic, to allow for it, and if we build it, it will come. My life isn't going to change if I just sit on the couch waiting—I need to get up and dance! I need to bring the party with me. Not wait for an invitation.

In the tango community there are certain women who when they walk in the room, all eyes turn to them. They enter with style, as if the force of their entire lives is walking in with them. The party starts when they arrive.

"*Know, first, who you are; and then adorn yourself accordingly.*"

—EPICTETUS

Picture this: It's about eleven P.M. on a Saturday night at El Encuentro, a weekly milonga (tango party) held in the Los Angeles area. All the die-hard tango dancers are just now beginning to show up (tango attracts a late-night crowd). A dark green vintage Rolls Royce pulls up and parks in front. A refined silver-haired gentleman in an elegantly cut black suit gets out of the car, walks over to the passenger side, and opens the door for his lady friend. She extends a black-gloved hand and allows her man to assist her as she emerges from the vehicle.

As she steps out we notice her shoes, high-heeled pumps encrusted with red Swarovski crystals; then, as she stands, we see her in all her fabulous sartorial glory. She is wearing a chic, floor-length aubergine velvet coat with a marabou collar, her hair is black and bobbed like the silent movie star Louise Brooks, her lips are painted Russian red, and she has a brilliant smile that could outshine the lights of Broadway. This is Das. And SHE'S NINETY-THREE YEARS OLD! That's style, baby—the kind of charm and allure that has no expiration date. And if that isn't magic I don't know what is.

## THE VIEW, TANGO STYLE

One night I was sitting at a milonga talking to some of the fantastic women I've met through dancing. (Sitting and talking with these women while waiting to dance is almost as fun and empowering as the dance itself.)

Julie Friedgen is a vivacious sixty-something screenwriter who owns the Tango Room dance center and co-hosts one of LA's most popular and long-running milongas, El Encuentro:

"When women start dancing, they change. When they start, they come in with their slacks, and a functional kind of blouse. A year later the same woman is wearing a tight skirt, fishnets, and she's lost twenty pounds. Because now she wants to fit into those cheap clothes that she wouldn't be caught dead in anywhere else!

You know if you go into Forever 21 and you see a woman over forty there, she's dancing tango."

Shannon Wilcox is an actress and former model, and at sixty-seven, she has a figure to rival a thirty-five-year-old. She wears her silver hair undyed and naturally beautiful and loves to dress in feminine body-conscious clothes:

"You know what? I put on a dress sometimes just to go to the grocery store. It's just that a dress makes me feel feminine, and then I walk with a little smile and then often someone stops me and says, 'I want what you've got right now!'"

Mila Vigdorova is a professional tanguera known for her grace and technical proficiency. A dark-haired Russian woman in her mid-thirties with classical features and a dancer's regal posture, when she enters a milonga, all eyes inevitably turn toward her:

"I think sometimes women neglect their physical beauty because they think that it is too superficial—the elegance, the beauty. But the beauty I am talking about is not your pretty face or the idea that you should dye your hair or paint your nails. It's how you carry yourself. Beauty is something that is not superficial to me, it is internal—this kind of beauty is something much deeper. It's a kind of self-respect. This is something that Russian women know very well how to do because my mom's generation—they didn't have much, they couldn't buy fashionable clothes because they weren't available to them. So they had to be super creative,

> *"It doesn't matter how big, how old, how pretty, et cetera, you are. The most important thing to convey is your attitude—that you 'like yourself.' People will notice and ask you to dance."*
>
> —DANA FRÍGOLI, PROFESSIONAL TANGUERA,
> OWNER, DNI TANGO, BUENOS AIRES

to find something to make themselves different, to make themselves stand out, to make themselves feel beautiful. So they learned to create these things out of nothing. And it's not the beauty that the feminist movement was fighting against, it's not the beauty to please the man—man's most stupid version of what a woman should look like—because when a man loves you, he loves you because of you; because you have your own special beauty. And it comes from inside of you."

> *"I think they should have a Barbie with a buzz cut."*
>
> —ELLEN DEGENERES

The other day I was watching the popular daytime talk show *The View* and I noticed how all five of the show's hosts really have their own special style. Barbara Walters always looks very professional and old-school elegant in beautifully cut dresses

ABOVE: *My feet in my very first pair of Comme Il Fauts. (This brand is considered the Jimmy Choo of tango shoes. Yum.)*

LEFT: *This is my foot in my favorite practice shoe. (Custom-made by Georges Dance Shoes of Burbank, California.)*

and suits. Elisabeth Hasselbeck dresses youthfully with her long blond hair and slightly frilly blouses and skirts. Joy Behar dresses simply but wears her hair red and spiky and often sports oversized earrings. Sherri Shepherd loves her curly hair and fun bright colors and always looks great. But for me, Whoopi Goldberg is the most stylish. Like Diane Keaton with her hats and oversized menswear looks, Katharine Hepburn with her ubiquitous slacks and high-necked blouses, Ellen DeGeneres with her boyish sneakers, short hair, slacks, and shirts, Whoopi is an iconoclast; she has a style utterly her own. Those round glasses and those crazy dreads, the oversized man-tailored shirts and vests over simple black pants and jeans. And on this particular show she was wearing a pair of shiny silver tennis shoes attached with what looked like iridescent *angel wings.* This is a woman who thinks about her appearance, she obviously doesn't just throw her clothes on in the morning—she definitely has a personal style and I think she always looks fabulous.

So my point is that you don't need to wear tons of makeup, a slit skirt, and high heels to dress like a goddess. While it's absolutely fine (and sometimes a lot of fun!) to throw on a sequined miniskirt and a red lace corset and go take a pole-dancing class, it's equally fabulous to put on some old jeans and cowboys boots and go out Texas two-stepping—you get to define your goddess's vestments for yourself.

> "*For* women, there are only three ages in Hollywood: Babe, D.A. [District Attorney], and Driving Miss Daisy."
>
> —GOLDIE HAWN

I've been told that I look good for my age. I inherited great genes from my parents, I exercise faithfully, watch what I eat, and am a sunscreen fanatic. But while I may look great for fifty I don't look thirty. And if I try to present myself that way, wear the clothes and makeup I did at thirty, I look like a fool. Style-wise, I am way past miniskirts, puff sleeves, and ruffles. So, even though I'm still a size four and might be able to squeeze myself into a latex dress, it doesn't mean it's the right look for me. Just because I *can*, doesn't mean I *should*.

We've all seen women who try desperately (and the key word here is *desperately*) to hold on to what they looked like in their twenties and thirties. You see it everywhere out here in Hollywood, all those trout-lipped, Botoxed, big-bosomed Hugh Hefner–type blondes. They turn themselves into these kind of Franken-women—they don't look young, they just look, well, weird. And the sad thing is that they not only ruin their faces, but their careers.

I have a few friends who are "movie stars"—a couple of them have been nominated for an Academy Award, the whole deal. The thing that these ladies have in common (besides the fact that they are all incredibly smart, talented, and funny!) is that they are all over forty-five, are celebrated beauties, and haven't succumbed to drastic surgery to preserve their good looks.

One time one of my movie star friends and I were discussing

our transition from babe to *post*-babe, and she told me that someone once asked her if it was hard to see all the younger actresses
coming up and receiving the fame she once enjoyed. She said no,
that she had her fair share of time in the spotlight, and that all
these young women . . . "need moms." I mean, when a forty-five-
year-old beauty starts looking like the Joker in a blond wig, what
role is she going to play? Does *your* mother look like that?

# THE SCARVES AND
# TURTLENECK YEARS

I have some friends and acquaintances who've had plastic surgery.
And some of them look great. But the one thing that they all agree
on is this: While they may have liked the look of their eyes or
their neck a little better after the surgeries, they still didn't like
*themselves* more afterward. If they were consumed with angst or
low self-esteem before the surgery, the improvements to their outward appearance didn't change that. They told me the surgery
didn't "fix" those feelings, that they felt just as insecure after the
surgery as before. They realized, like the old adage, that beauty
really is an inside job.

Having said that, I'm still human. I have headshots and film
footage of myself from age six to fifty, and believe me, I notice the
changes in my face, and, I'll be honest, I hate the way my neck
looks. I have a burn scar on my throat from a childhood injury
and while it was very unnoticeable for most of my life, it has become very pronounced as I have gotten older. One side of my
throat looks fifty and the other looks eighty. My solution? I
DON'T LOOK AT MY NECK! Really! I just focus on areas

of my face that I like and figure the hell with the rest. A form of denial? Maybe. But you know what? It works. It's like that old song "accentuate the positive." I find that if I carry myself as if I *feel* beautiful, if I focus on my assets instead of my flaws, that feeling emanates out into the world. And when I have to go before the cameras? (I know, I say it like I'm going before the executioners.) It's scarves and turtlenecks, baby—scarves and turtlenecks! (But, I might throw on a feather boa from time to time, just to let the kids know I'm still in the game.)

## GIVE A GOOD DANCE

There is a certain very famous movie star (now happily married) who used to be notorious for his sexual conquests (with very little effort you can probably figure out who I'm talking about). He's incredibly handsome and talented, but in Hollywood that's not really all that uncommon. What really seems to set this guy apart from the pack, and why he's still magnetically attractive at well past seventy, is his *charm.*

I know a few of the women he used to date, and several people who have worked with him or know him socially. And each person describes him in the same way. They all say, "When you're with him, he treats you like you're the most important person in the room. Like nothing or no one could be as fascinating as you." And they all agree he's the most charming person they have ever met.

So how do we develop charm? I have a friend who instead of the ubiquitous expression, "Have a good day," has as the greeting on his voice mail, "*Give* a good day." I believe that charming people understand that to *have* a good day, you have to *give* one.

I used to hate the holidays. I always missed the wonder and joy I experienced as a child, when I'd be sleepless with anticipation on Christmas Eve wondering what I'd find under the tree for me the next morning after Santa had made his visit. Then later, as an adult with no children, I felt a sense of longing, a feeling of emptiness, which would often tip into acute self-pity.

But one year I decided to volunteer with an organization that provides holiday meals and toys for needy families, and everything changed. When I saw the look on a mother's face as I handed her a bag filled with the fixings for a huge turkey dinner with all the trimmings, and saw her tear up as her little ones received armloads of toys, I realized the truth of my friend's voice mail greeting, that the only way to really *have* a good day is to *give* one. And I've made volunteering at Christmastime a personal tradition ever since.

If you ever feel sad or lonely, go to a nursing home and find an elderly person with no living friends or relatives and make them feel like they are not alone. Next time you go grocery shopping, ask the checkout person how their day is going; if it's someone you see every time you go to the store, find out their name, and remember it. If you dance, make a guy who is just learning the tango feel like he's a great leader and should stick with it. If you go out to *give* a good day, I guarantee that you'll find the true meaning of the season whether it's Christmastime or not.

Anyone in a long-term relationship knows that sometimes it can be tough to always remember to treat your partner with the appreciation and respect he deserves—passion ebbs, bills and health problems crop up, the normal challenges of life wreak their havoc. So every day I make a conscious decision to remember my guy's good qualities. Every morning, when I wake up, even before I open my eyes, I do a little meditation. I say a little prayer that my presence in his life makes my man feel better about who he is in the world—that I do whatever I can to make his life better. Then I try to do what I can to make him feel as loved as he is.

On the dance floor, so much of my enjoyment is dictated by my attitude. Maybe a man asked me to dance who I've heard is a bad leader, but I've been waiting for a while to be asked for a dance, so I begrudgingly join him on the floor. At first, I'm resistant to his lead because I have preconceived notions about his ability. But, after a minute or two, he surprises me. I discover that actually he's a *wonderful* dancer! Conversely, maybe I am asked to dance by someone I believe to be a "master," maybe a teacher or someone fresh from studying in Buenos Aires, so I assume they're great—a much better dancer than I am. And if that partner throws me off balance, or his lead is too rough, or even if he steps on my foot, I'll immediately blame myself. But at one point I will finally realize that this guy doesn't know what he's doing! In both of these cases, I have come to the dance with preconceived ideas and judgments, and in both cases my attitude influences what kind of experience I'll have.

I need to come to each new partner with an open mind and heart. And to do this, the best thing I can do is set my default position to "Give a good dance."

> "*Some people, no matter how old they get, never lose their beauty—they merely move it from their faces into their hearts.*"
>
> —MARTIN BUXBAUM, WRITER

One night at a milonga I noticed an older couple dancing a waltz. Both partners looked to be in their mid-sixties, maybe older. The man was dressed in a dark well-cut pinstriped suit, his salt-and-pepper hair was cropped short, and he was clearly captivated by his partner. Her hair was long and gray and contrasted beautifully with her chestnut-colored skin. She wore an elegant black satin dress scattered here and there with silver sequins. Her black patent leather stiletto heels flashed as she executed her boleos (small kicks) and sweeps (leg brushes on the floor). She wasn't as technically proficient as many dancers I've seen, her feet didn't arch and point perfectly, and she was attempting some moves that were maybe a bit beyond her talent level, but I could see so clearly that she *felt* beautiful. And I couldn't take my eyes off her.

While she was obviously deeply connected to her partner, I knew she could feel my eyes on her and I could tell she was dancing a bit for me as well as for him. I was reminded of something the magnificent professional tanguera (female tango dancer) Silvina Valz once told me: that I should "dance for the man *behind* me" as well as for the one in front of me.

I could tell that my attention was feeding this woman's energy and it was making her dance better. She reminded me of a queen in her court whose presence commands the attention of everyone in the room, those behind her as well as those in front—knowing that all eyes are always upon her.

Off the dance floor this woman might be overlooked. She was certainly older than what is typically thought of by today's society as sexually desirable, but here, on the dance floor, she has a place where she can express the most glamorous and lyrical aspects of her femininity. She can wear a sequined dress, and flashy heels, and move with elegant sensuality. She can play in a land that her "regular" life might not allow. And her partner looked at her like she was the most beautiful woman in the room. Fred Astaire with Ginger Rogers. It brought tears to my eyes, for in this magical world of partner dance, there live housewives, supermarket cashiers, and lawyers by day, who are terpsichorean goddesses by night.

# EXERCISES FOR
# FINDING YOUR INNER GODDESS

First, get yourself a journal. You will use it for several of the exercises in this book and to chart your discoveries and/or dance progress.

### EXERCISE 1: CHANNELING YOUR INNER GODDESS

Now you get to begin thinking about how to become a tango goddess (or swing goddess, or salsa goddess, etc.). Or, if you don't dance, how to become a goddess in your everyday life.

It's best to do this exercise the last thing before you go to bed. Take out your journal and write the names of two women you admire. Women who for you embody the word "goddess." For me, this first list might include Michelle Obama and Helen Mirren. If you're a dancer, your list can include dancers you admire.

Under each woman's name, write five qualities she possesses that you find beautiful and reflective of her goddess nature. Don't worry if the qualities you write down make no sense (see my Helen Mirren list). Just write down the first five qualities that come into your head.

For me, the list might look like this: *continues*

## Michelle Obama

Brilliant • Strong • Stylish • Graceful
• Great arms

## Helen Mirren

Gorgeous • Sexually alive • Crow's feet/wrinkles
• Adventurous • Fiercely talented

Now close the journal. The next night, make the list again without referring to the list you made the night before. You can pick two new women, but it's also OK if you repeat the same names. Just make the list.

My second list might look like this:

## Whoopi Goldberg

Funny • Smart • Stylish • Self-possessed/exactly herself/comfortable in her own skin • Strong

## Julianne Moore

Talented • Freckles • Natural redhead • Smart
• Confident

Don't try to control what names make your list. Even if the names on your list don't make sense to your conscious mind, let your subconscious make its choices. If you are surprised by some of the names that come up, that's even better. You're discovering unexplored aspects of your innermost self—what kind of woman you want to be, what kind of women you admire. And actually you'll find out that this is the kind of woman, at least on some level, you already are.

Do this exercise every night for one week. Make sure that every night you don't look at what you wrote the night before. At the end of the week, look over all your entries. Pick your favorite two women from all your lists and your favorite five qualities from all your lists. Notice if the same quality repeats itself again and again. That means it's important to you. (The qualities do not have to be from the same women chosen as your two favorites). This new list is your goddess template. You will use it in future exercises.

*continues*

## EXERCISE 2: THE SHOPPING CART TANGO

The next time you go to the market (make sure to grab a shopping cart, not a basket) you're going to do a little dance called "The Shopping Cart Tango."

Grasp the handle lightly with both hands and start walking down an aisle. Slow your steps. Try to make each step the same size. Keep your stride length consistent. If they are playing music in the store, walk to that rhythm. If not, imagine your favorite dance song (slow is best) or bring an iPod. Try to feel like you and the shopping cart are one. That it's an extension of your body. Try to feel like you are walking in a kind of gliding movement. Enjoy this feeling. Like dancing. Now think of one of your goddesses. How would she walk right now? Do this exercise as if you were an eight-year-old child playing a game. Just pretend. It doesn't matter if it is perfect or "good." Just have fun with it. Now try the other goddess. Or just try on one of your favorite goddess "qualities." For example, "gracefulness." See how graceful you can make your walk. Do this and all the other exercises as often as you like. A goddess always feels free to "dabble."

*chapter three*

## L Is for *Listen*

*"If speaking is silver, then*

*listening is gold."*

—TURKISH PROVERB

When I was first learning to dance the tango, my teacher did an exercise that showed me what it was like to really listen to your partner. He brought two huge kitchen knives to our practice that night. Then he handed me one of the knives and he held the other. We clasped each other's wrists, his right, my left, and faced each other. Our free hands held the knives and pointed them directly toward each other. I felt like we were about to have a knife fight. Suddenly my attention shot from 50 percent to 100 percent! My teacher made his point (pun intended) in about two seconds flat. He said, "This is what it feels like to really pay attention to your partner."

I said, "Got it. Um, I kind of feel like I'm in a horror movie, can we put the knives down now?"

Of course what my teacher was trying to show me with that exercise was that to really dance with a partner in a fully connected way, I needed to learn how to listen as if my life depended on it. So, the first concept in the principle of L.O.V.E. is to learn how to really *listen*.

*"Anyone who is able to waltz, or fox-trot, or tango, or perform any sort of dance that requires physical contact with a responsive partner, knows that there is a first moment, on the dance floor, when you assess, automatically, whether the new partner in question can dance at all."*

—MICHAEL CUNNINGHAM, WRITER

When I dance with a new partner, in those first moments as we face each other on the floor waiting for the music to begin, I practice a kind of *active* listening. I try to empty my mind of everything. Then, I try to become hyper-aware of all my senses. I notice the level of light in the room. I feel the energy and sound of the people around me on the dance floor. I notice the temperature and how it feels on my skin. I am friendly and open to my partner, but I don't do a lot of talking. If he's talking, introducing himself, etc., I'm polite. I answer his questions, I nod my head, but I am a woman of few words.

What I want to do is really be present in that moment so I can be available to really *hear*—with my whole body—his lead. He raises his arms—I place my left arm around his shoulder and my right hand in his left. I let him set the embrace, the proximity of our bodies (whether it's an open or closed embrace). I don't grab or lean my weight on him. I am connected to him, but still in charge of my own balance. I take my time. I breathe. I want to feel this moment before the movement starts for as long as I can. I want to try to understand how this person communicates.

I've learned to practice this same type of *active* listening off the dance floor as well. I can't tell you how many times I've been able to be more loving with my guy, or with a girlfriend, by in effect *feeling* what they're saying instead of just listening to their words.

Elliott Jaffa, Ed.D., a behavioral psychologist who regularly conducts "active listening" seminars for businesses and other groups, says, "In reality, very few people really know how to listen. There's more to active listening than sitting back and letting your eardrum collect vibrations. When done properly, it's actually hard work. It's almost like learning another language, but as many truly good listeners have discovered, the rewards are worth it." According to Dr. Jaffa, active listening requires at least one hundred different learned behaviors, but a couple of his tips to becoming a better listener are "Stop talking. Silence is the key to listening" and "Send the right signals. Show respect by giving your full attention."

I remember once talking to one of my favorite leaders, Vladimir Estrin, a professional tango teacher and performer and founder of the popular tango resource website, tangoafficionado .com. He told me that for him the best part of the dance is the connection between the two people. And because of that, he especially loves dancing with beginners. He feels that because they are so new to the dance, they have no preconceived notions and as a result are sometimes more willing to connect—more open to him and his lead than someone who has been dancing for a long time. He says that a follower who is a more sophisticated dancer might sometimes just go through the motions of the dance while her mind is elsewhere. He said, "If I look at my partner's face and she is looking across the room at something or someone else while we are dancing, it's over for me."

Does this sound familiar? I've experienced it at many a Hollywood cocktail party. You'll be talking with someone and they'll keep looking over your shoulder to see if there's someone more important than you in the room. I, for one, don't particularly want to spend time with this type of person, and most important, I don't want to *be* this type of person.

Listening may seem passive, but it's not; in fact, it's almost the opposite. In many ways, being the listener requires more energy and concentration than being the one who does all the talking.

Think about a time when you really felt "heard" in a conversation. Was the person just sitting there, staring at you with a blank face? Were they looking around the room while you were talking? No. Even if they just let you talk, with no interruptions, you could probably almost feel their attention. When someone is *actively* listening to you it feels like an exchange of energy. It's like they are really receiving the energy, the feeling, of what you have to say, and sending it back to you, without saying a word. They may nod their head, or their eyes may tear up, or they may smile, but they are fully present with you.

Although the goal is eventually to improvise, when you first learn to dance—whether it's salsa, tango, or swing—you begin by learning a series of basic steps. Once you have mastered

> "*Dance* is like learning a new language. It reminds me of when I was visiting Italy and I would try to understand. I would listen and then I really had to think about what they were saying, not just assume. So I learned that if I just kept my mouth shut and listened, then I would think, 'OK, this is what I am translating it to mean' and then I would reply and if they understood me I would think, 'Great, I translated it correctly!' That was the 'aha' moment for me: Sit back, be quiet, don't be so critical, don't presume anything, just listen."
>
> —VERONICA, SALSA DANCER

these, you move on to more advanced patterns. It's very similar to learning a new language: First you have to learn the basic words and phrases before you can have an actual conversation.

Having said that, even though in lead/follow dances you have to know the steps, the follower must be able to recognize the lead, but not *anticipate* it. The trick when receiving a lead is not to go into a kind of oh-I-know-this-pattern-because-I-learned-it-in-dance-class-last-week autopilot and dance like a windup toy who does her dance this way and *only* this way, but rather for the fol-

> " *When* you're following, it's really an adventure to see
> what he's going to do. You know, to wait and see, what is
> he going to lead me through. What kind of a ride is he
> going to take me on?"
>
> —LAURA CANELLIAS,
> PROFESSIONAL SALSA TEACHER AND DANCER

lower to listen in an *active* way—she must "hear" (through her body) the lead and then execute it in a way that is open for improvisation.

This kind of "active listening" is difficult, but it's how the magic happens. If you listen in a way that is open to change, even though you may be doing the same basic steps or dancing to a song you've heard over and over before, it's always going to feel like a new adventure with every partner.

Sometimes it's even harder to listen actively when you're dancing with one of your regular partners. Just like any long-term relationship, you get to the point where you feel like you can finish each other's sentences, you can become so used to dancing with one person that you can easily fall into the trap of assuming you know what they are going to do every moment without really paying attention. You think to yourself, "Oh, Joe always leads a double turn-out spin after that step," so your body goes right into the turn before he's even led it. While in some ways it's wonderful to know someone so well that you get to the point where you can, in fact, finish each other's sentences—there is a great feeling of comfort and security in familiarity—that doesn't mean you should. On or off the dance floor, you don't want to become so used to your partner's habits that you take them for granted. You always have to be open to the possibility that your partner may grow. You're not the same person you were yesterday, and neither is your partner.

Another common problem with followers is what dancers call "back leading" or "highjacking" the lead. This is when the follower sort of goes rogue. She's not listening to her partner—she's dancing her own dance; she's doing whatever she feels like in spite of his lead.

Dancing with a follower like this is like having a conversation with someone who only talks about themselves. It's not only rude, it's boring. Obviously a leader will not want to dance with a follow like this. When dancing with her, he will feel disrespected and alone.

But you know who may really be missing out? The follower. Her leader may have been planning to take her on the dance floor equivalent of a trip to Paris in the springtime, yet she highjacked the journey to Bakersfield in high summer. Where would *you* rather dance?

# I'M TALKING SO LOUD, I CAN'T HEAR WHAT YOU'RE SAYING

Before I began partner dancing, I didn't know how to really listen. For one thing, I was a chronic interrupter. I meant well, but I was like that annoying kid in class who shoots their hand up as soon as a question comes out of the teacher's mouth: "Me! Me! Pick me!"

I didn't mean to be rude; I would just get excited by an idea and feel that I had to blurt it out. It was like I felt that if I didn't get what I had to say out that very second, I would never have another chance.

Or sometimes I would get impatient. I'm a very energetic person. If I were a drink at Starbucks I'd be a double espresso, not a decaf green tea soy latte. I'm a fast thinker—my mind works very quickly. Now don't misunderstand me, I'm not saying that I am necessarily a *smart* thinker, but I'm *fast*. And sometimes it gets me into trouble. I tend to rush into things—I often speak before I think.

The upside of this aspect of my personality is that I'm very passionate and adventurous. I'm always willing to dive in and try something new (like the Argentine tango, for example). And because I can't sit still—I'm always moving around with a kind of self-generating hyper-energy like one of those little Jack Russell dogs that are constantly jumping up and down—I'm thin.

But there is a downside to having this kind of intense energy. I tend to be impulsive. I'll sometimes commit to things that I later regret, and I can get impatient with people who have a slower energy. I'll often be thinking, "OK, let's hurry things along here, let's get to the point already!"

And in the way that relationships always seem to end up providing the perfect conditions to enable you to work on your own character defects, my guy is handsome, intelligent, funny, and a *very* slow talker. It drives me crazy. It's like the old adage: If you need to learn patience, God gives you long lines.

Before I started practicing the principles of L.O.V.E. when my guy and I were having a conversation, I would find myself wanting to kind of hurry things along. I would say things like: "Yeah, yeah, got it! I know where you're going with this," and then interrupt with what I thought he was going to say. I would assume, rather than really listen. But you know what? I wasn't always right. In fact, I was often dead wrong.

## A MAN CAN HANDLE
## HIS OWN MEATBALLS

Recently my husband and I had dinner at a local Italian restaurant. When the waiter came to take our order, my guy ordered spaghetti and meatballs. When our food came, the waiter set down in front of my husband a steaming plate of pasta with thick marinara sauce—*but no meatballs.*

"Didn't you order spaghetti with meatballs?" I asked.

"Yes, I did," my guy replied, looking down at his plate.

I waited for a moment, assuming he'd call the waiter over to tell him about the mistake. But instead, he did nothing.

"Well, where are the meatballs?" I asked. Thinking to myself: "He's not doing anything. I have to fix this! I must flag down that absentminded waiter and demand that he provide my husband with his meatballs! Immediately!"

But, thankfully, at this point I had been dancing for a few years, and I remembered to practice the concept of active listening. I paused, bit my tongue, and then the thought came to me, "My husband is a grown man, and he is perfectly capable of handling his own meatballs." So, instead of resorting to my old take-charge, I-need-to-fix-this-situation behavior (without having been asked to, I might add), I took a deep breath and started in on my own meal.

A moment later, my guy, with a gentle nod of his head, signaled the waiter to come to the table. When the young man arrived, my husband said: "Um, do you have meatballs?"

"Yes, sir, we do. Would you like me to bring you a side order?" (Obviously the waiter had misheard my guy's original order.)

My husband thought for a moment, and then he said: "You know what? I don't need meatballs. I'm fine with what I have. "

One more time, a lesson learned. I may think I know where my partner is going on the dance floor (or what my guy is going to order in a restaurant), but he just may surprise me.

Also, it's not my job to "fix things" because much of the time they're not broken. And even when they are, I have to remember that my husband is perfectly capable of handling his own meatballs. And he's most definitely fine with what he has. (And incidentally, so am I.)

# IF IT'S HYSTERICAL,
# IT'S HISTORICAL

There's a great expression: "If it's hysterical, it's historical." What this means is, when I'm *really* upset about something, it often indicates I'm being reminded of something that happened in my past. For example, it may *look* like I'm having a fight with my guy, but *emotionally* I'm eight years old on the playground crying because that little blond girl I so admired didn't pick me to be on her softball team.

*"Pick your battles."*

—MY MOTHER (AND EVERY OTHER WOMAN WHO'S
EVER BEEN IN A LONG-TERM RELATIONSHIP)

For as long as I can remember, I've been very sensitive—almost unbearably so. And since kids will be kids, from an early age I was constantly teased about my red hair. My mom used to tell me that when I was being bullied the best thing for me to do was to call out, "Sticks and stones may break my bones but names will never hurt me!" But, of course, that's not true; words *do* hurt. So early on I learned to cover my tears with feistiness. From at least age eight, I've been leading with my chin. And I've brought that feisty energy not only to the dance floor but to every area of my life.

Even when I first studied yoga, I started out with good intentions; I wanted to find a way to relax and meditate. But then I discovered Power Yoga, and soon my yoga practice became more about dropping down and doing forty *chaturangas* (yoga push-ups) than sitting in lotus position and chanting, "Om." For me, even if it was only with myself, everything was a competition.

So, being who I am, after I'd been dancing for a while I sometimes got into dance fights. Don't get me wrong, I'm speaking metaphorically of course. I mean, I wouldn't actually pound some unsuspecting leader with a solid left hook (although believe me, there were plenty of times when I was tempted).

When I was a beginning dancer, I was much better at going with the flow. I hadn't yet become an "expert." Everything was wonderful and new. I would dance with other beginners, or those slightly more advanced, and it was like the blind leading (or following) the blind. I wasn't yet sophisticated enough in my dancing to disapprove of anything. I was like a little baby crawling around, checking everything out with an open mind, happily eating leaves or dirt and finding them delicious. To me, every dance was an exciting new adventure.

But once I reached the intermediate level in my dancing—what I call "my teen years"—and thought I knew what I was doing, like a hormonally challenged teenage girl, my "stuff" started coming up. I became arrogant and disapproving. I danced with a chip on my shoulder. If a guy was rough with his lead, or didn't allow me the time to finish completing a movement before he moved on to the next one, I would take it as a personal affront. I always came from a place that he was doing it intentionally. I never gave my leaders the benefit of the doubt. I came to the dance floor with an attitude of, "Show me what you've got, mister, and I'll tell you if I like it!"

For instance, I used to be in a dance class with a guy I'll call

> *"At some point you will step onto the dance floor and meet yourself."*
>
> —VLADIMIR ESTRIN,
> PROFESSIONAL TANGUERO

"Frank." He drove me crazy. I couldn't stand dancing with him. He had a sort of hard-core military buzz cut and a very stern expression. He looked to me just like the kind of person I'd avoid socially. I made all kinds of surface judgments about him because of the way he looked. I assumed we had nothing in common—that he was Mister Gun-toting Military Guy to my free-spirited *artiste.*

In this particular class we'd make a circle and rotate partners and I would always feel my body tense as I saw my turn to dance with Frank drawing near. It was like inside I was saying, "Force fields UP!"

When he would finally, inevitably, arrive at my spot in the circle, I would smile politely and rigidly accept his dance embrace. I gave him not one inch of error. If he didn't lead in the way I thought was correct, I would resist, and my displeasure was *very* apparent. I wouldn't overtly roll my eyes, but I was definitely rolling them on the inside. And I know he could feel it. I would just judge the hell out of him. And you know, I'm ashamed to say, it gave me a feeling of power. It made me feel superior.

When Frank and I came together on the dance floor, it felt

more like we were going to arm wrestle or box than dance the tango.

I would say "helpful" little things such as "I don't think you led that right" or "That's not the move the teacher asked us to practice." I would be like the person in the passenger seat of the car saying little nagging things to the driver like "You should have turned left there" or "Don't you think you should go around that car?" or "Could you please drive a little slower?" or "Aren't you following that guy ahead a little close?" (Not that I have ever done anything like that on a road trip with my husband, you understand . . .)

Well, surprise, surprise, my "helping" never seemed to help Frank one bit. In fact, it always seemed to make things worse. Now, if someone just heard my *words*, they might have seemed innocent enough. But I was saying them with an inner aggression— my inner intention was to say, "You are wrong. You don't know what you're doing. You are a terrible leader and on top of that, I don't like your haircut!" and I knew that Frank could feel it.

Soon, in a weird way, I would almost look forward to dancing with Frank. It began to feel like a challenge. In the same way that sometimes driving in LA can be exciting and challenging in a weird way. "AHA! You think you can pass me? Well, watch this!" Like Ali *vs.* Frazier I would literally go toe-to-toe with Frank, challenging him energetically to lead me successfully through whatever move we were currently working on.

One night in class, things came to a head. Frank, frustrated when I didn't move in the direction he was trying to indicate with his lead, pointed and said, "I want you to move *there!*"

I instantly got my back up and said, "How dare you talk

to me like that! Like I'm your dog and you're commanding me to sit!"

And he retorted, "Well a dog would obey!"

And I got furiously indignant and stormed out of the class.

Soon, I found myself standing in the hall, weeping. Frank ran after me.

"I'm sorry!" he exclaimed, "I am so sorry!" And he looked at me with such concern, it took me aback.

"Uh, it's OK, I'm OK . . ."

"No, it's not OK," he replied. "That was a terrible thing for me to say. It's just that, you're such a good dancer, and I want you to *like* to dance with me and, well, I know I can get intense."

And I felt like I had awakened from a dream. One of those nightmarish ones where you want to scream and can't make a sound. Only this time I was screaming when there really was no cause to. The reason I had been feeling a need to scream didn't, in fact, exist. I felt my whole body relax, and I realized that I was fighting a battle that was within me. It had nothing to do with Frank.

"Oh, Frank," I said, "no, it's really OK, *I'm* intense too. Believe me."

And Frank said, "Oh, I believe you!" and we both laughed.

It felt like we had the shared realization that we were both a couple of control freaks working our problems out on the dance floor.

And I said, "God, look at us! It's just dancing—it's *dancing*! It's supposed to be *fun*!"

And he said, "Yeah, I know."

And then he looked down at his feet for a moment as if considering and said, "I have a military background, and back then, when I gave an order it really was life or death, I couldn't show any weakness or misgiving. So now, I don't know, in dancing, it's just so hard for me to lighten up. Everything just always feels like life and death to me."

I felt like a real heel. I had totally misjudged this guy. He had pressures inside of him and probably memories I could never imagine.

And then he went on, "And honestly, you know how I always seem tense when we dance? One time I was at El Encuentro and I had been dancing for about an hour and a half, and was feeling like I was looking really good. I was feeling really proud of my leading. And then I sat down and looked at my lap and discovered that my fly had been open the whole time. And now, whenever I'm near a pretty girl at a milonga or a class, if I realize that I haven't checked my fly lately, I get really nervous. I don't want to look down at my crotch in the middle of a dance right in front of her. So then all I'm thinking about is how worried I am that my fly might be open the whole time I'm dancing with her."

When he said that, I just melted. I had decided he was so rigid when he danced because he was mean, that he didn't like me. And the whole time he had been worried about his fly!

If I'd been really *listening* to Frank—if I'd been really *present* with him instead of living up in my own head, I might have seen earlier that Frank was a lot like me. His stern-looking exterior was just like my "feistiness"—a tool we both used to mask our extreme sensitivity. After that experience with Frank, I learned that it was time to stop leading with my chin, that actually I was much happier when I was willing to lead with my heart.

## REPEAT AFTER ME

Dr. Nicki Monti, an old friend of mine, is a well-known therapist and relationship expert here in Los Angeles. I spoke to her about the idea of *active* listening and she told me of a classic therapeutic tool she uses when working with couples called "repeat and respond."

In this process you actually *repeat* what the other person has just said, either silently in your head, or out loud. For example, "I hear you're saying 'X,'" or "You'd like me to do 'X.'" She told me that this is the "oldest tool in couples' work . . . repeat and respond, repeat and respond. It's a very simple process . . . and *no one does it*!"

Why do we forget to do it? Well, speaking for myself, I've found that when I'm triggered emotionally, I tend to kind of "flee the scene"—I forget everything around me and retreat to my brain. Then, I'm no longer having a conversation with the person in front of me, but am living in my own head. Even though to an outside observer it may *look* like I'm fighting with my guy, actually I might be reliving an argument I had with my mother when I was thirteen years old, or even eight—licking my wounds over being called one of those "names that never hurt."

So whenever I get really mad or really sad, it's very important that I remember to stay in the present and keep *listening*—I need to, as Ram Dass said, "Be here now." To do that, first I need to remember to *breathe*. It may sound simple but just concentrating on my breath gets me back in the present and gives me a chance to *pause,* both verbally and *emotionally.* Remember that old adage that when you're angry, you should count to ten before you speak? Well, taking a few deep breaths is my version of that. Then once I'm sure I'm back in the present moment, I try to "repeat," either to myself or aloud, what the person I'm in conflict with has said before I even think of my response.

I've rarely regretted the things I've left unsaid when I remembered to pause and hold my tongue, but I sure have regretted many of the things I've said in anger. If I make my first priority to *listen,* if I remember to take a breath and *pause* before I speak, I stand a much better chance of actually having a conversation with the person in front of me, as opposed to that person who lives in my head. I also have a much better chance of using my words in a way that helps rather than harms.

# IF YOU DON'T TRY TO FIX IT— YOU *JUST* MAY FIND OUT THAT IT WORKS

What if you're dancing with a leader who's not leading well? His lead is rough, or unclear, or maybe he's new to dancing and is attempting some moves that are beyond his skill level. What's the best thing you can do to help? DON'T TRY TO FIX IT! If you do try to fix it, most of the time you will just make it worse. Why? Because you're not a mind reader. If you try to assume or imagine what a leader is trying to lead you through, you will get into the habit of anticipating. You will be in your head instead of being in the moment. Then, next time you're dancing with a great leader, you might try to "fix it" again and end up highjacking the lead.

Or let's say your leader is a beginner, and a really nice person, and you really think you know exactly what he is trying to lead you into. Now hear this! You are not doing him a favor by doing the movement when he doesn't lead it correctly. If he wants to improve, he needs your honest feedback. It's like sex, if you fake your orgasms, your guy will never learn how to give you a real one.

Once I was dancing with a leader who accused me of being "mean" to him because I was not fixing it for him. He was a very accomplished swing dancer but new to the tango. He was frustrated that his skill level wasn't such that he could lead the moves he saw others doing on the dance floor, and instead of being humble and learning how to lead the steps, he blamed it on *me*. This is like having a relationship with a guy who is angry and unhappy all the time and then tells you it's *your* fault—that if only you would cook better, or look better, or be nicer to him or whatever he comes up with, then he wouldn't feel so bad. Someone who does this is a bad partner, in dance and in life.

When I am actively listening, when I make it my business to simply follow my partner's lead, I am empowering him. I am giving my leader the gift of my respect and attention. I'm doing him the favor of not behaving like I'm his teacher, or worse, his mother. If a guy wants me to spin myself around doing fancy moves so he looks good on the dance floor when his lead hasn't earned it, he is in effect asking me to dance alone. And then why do I need him?

# SHALL WE DANCE?

In the milongas of Argentina there is a ritual called the cabeceo.

You are in a crowded milonga in Buenos Aires. You look up and notice a handsome tanguero (male tango dancer) looking at you. If you like him, you meet his gaze and hold it. He does a subtle nod of his head toward the dance floor—this is the cabeceo. Now you have a choice: You can either nod back, indicating your acceptance of his invitation, or look away. If you look away, he knows that his invitation has been rejected and he moves on.

This ritual is nice for both parties involved. The man doesn't have to walk across a crowded room to ask you to dance and risk a public rejection. And you get to say no in a graceful and subtle way, without fear of being unkind.

So who's the one in charge here? *You.* He has risked rejection, but the potential pain of that is worth it to him for the chance to dance with you. He wants you so much that he's willing to put himself out there. So you're really the one with the power. The "power" to ask a person to dance is actually in many ways the weaker position.

Luiza Paes, another gorgeous raven-haired goddess of the dance floor, is based in Buenos Aires and is a sought-after teacher internationally.

"In Argentine tango the roles are established so that men are in charge of navigating and women are in charge of keeping the connection. But in order to keep a connection, you have to be *of-fered* a connection. If you try to force the connection by going over and asking a man to dance, you're stepping into the masculine role. You're making it happen, but it's not in a female way. Think of the cabeceo. It is the method here in Buenos Aires, and it's not that the man asks the woman or even vice versa, but that they ask each other, through the eyes. If I want to dance with him, I will look at him. And my look at him will be my request. And then he will have the chance to say yes or no through looking back in the same way, and then asking me with the gesture of his head. And it's not important who starts looking first—that's not the point—but it's who *talks* first. The verbal communication, the walking over to the person, it has a different level—it's much more assertive—it's more definite about who is in charge. So if a woman walks over to a man and asks him to dance, she's taking on a lot of archetypical masculinity.

I think when we women dance the follower's role in tango, we are exercising our femininity. And being feminine is, I think, a *subtle* way of doing things. And I think this subtlety is something that is very nice for us to explore. And it's very feminine to make someone think they're asking us when actually we are asking them. What I mean by this is that I'm asking him by looking at him. It's subtle. Because I'm not assertively asking him, "Will you dance with me?" but instead, by looking at him, I'm making myself available to be asked.

In the animal world, it's the female that chooses the male, but she doesn't choose by grabbing him and saying, "You're going to be mine now!" But she's the one who, in the end, says, "Yes, I accept you," or "No, I don't accept you." Likewise, when you look at a guy, you are making yourself available for the invitation, so you're not being completely passive there at all, it's very active. But it's not a masculine kind of active, it's a feminine kind of active."

> "*In* America, women at the milongas go up to men
> and ask them to dance. And this is something I would
> never *do*. If you go ask him to dance, then you don't get
> to have this beautiful feeling that he chose you to dance
> with. If you ask him you will never be sure. Also, if you
> ask him to dance you have to be prepared to hear 'no,'
> and this is something that we women don't have to
> experience, because we women make ourselves available
> to dance and they *have to hear the 'no.' Right?*"
>
> —MILA VIGDOROVA, PROFESSIONAL TANGUERA

There is absolutely nothing wrong with asking a man to dance. However, you have to accept that you may be turned down. I've seen women get really indignant when they get rejected after asking a man to dance. But that was their choice. If a woman wants to step into the traditional male role of the leader, then she has to take the good with the bad. If she gets rejected, she must "take it like a man."

Whatever your individual choice is on this issue is fine. But know this: Just as you may be missing a wonderful adventure if you don't "listen" to a man's lead when you're dancing, by not letting him be the one to ask you for a dance you're missing a really beautiful feeling.

## YOU TALKIN' TO ME?

I remember the first time a man gave me the cabeceo. He was Argentine. I had seen him often at my regular milongas and he was a great dancer. On this particular night I looked up and saw him across the room looking at me with a friendly smile. I smiled back. Then he nodded his head at me. I wasn't quite sure what was happening—was this the famous cabeceo I'd heard about? I wasn't sure, and I also wasn't sure he was looking at me, and I didn't want to make a fool of myself, so I looked behind me and then back at him, then pointed at myself and mouthed "Me?"

I think he knew I was a beginner because he came closer so I couldn't mistake his intention and then again nodded his head toward the dance floor. I still wasn't sure, so I said, "Are you asking me to dance?" He bowed slightly, reached out his hand, and said, in a most charming and gentlemanly way, "No, I'm *begging* you to dance."

## SHALL WE DATE?

Back in my single days, years before I met my husband, I used to date like a guy. What I mean by that is that I would in effect play the "leader's" role in the relationship. If I met a guy I liked, I would call him up and ask him out. And even sometimes after a first date, if it went well, rather than wait and see if he picked up the ball and asked me again, I'd call him.

I prided myself on what I believed was my confident, take-no-prisoners dating style. "Hey, I don't have to wait for a guy to call *me*! I'm as perfectly capable of picking up the phone as he is, why should I *play games*?" But the fact is, I was being dishonest. I preferred the role of the aggressor, not because I was so confident, but because it scared me to let a relationship unfold without pushing it along. I was afraid that if I didn't *make* a relationship happen, it wouldn't.

After a first date with a new guy I liked, I'd be riddled with anxiety. What if he didn't like me? What if he doesn't call? I couldn't stand that feeling of waiting. And as much as I hated to admit it, I was, in fact, *waiting*. I may have looked like I was running around doing my life, but I was checking my voice mail every ten minutes.

At that time in my life I felt like I wasn't complete unless I was in a relationship (I hadn't yet found my "inner goddess"). And I felt like if I didn't muscle it, if I didn't try to control the outcome, if I in effect left room to "listen" to the behavior of the guy I was dating, I might find out that he was, to use a phrase from a popular self-help book, "just not that into me."

So I did the dating equivalent of walking across a dance floor and asking a guy to dance, rather than making myself available to be asked. And not only did I keep myself from experiencing the pleasure of being the one who was invited, but, after a certain point, I realized that my style was attracting the wrong kind of man. I wasn't attracting men who liked to "lead," men who enjoyed doing the courting, because I never gave them time to! Instead, I was attracting guys who preferred the "follower's" role.

If a guy stuck around through my aggressive dating style, it usually meant he liked it that way. Let's say that at one point I got tired of doing all the work; I'd stop calling, planning our dates, pushing our relationship along, and then I'd notice that when I stopped, he didn't start. I'd realize at that point that the person I had gotten involved with was very happy playing the role of the "follower" in the dance of our relationship. Then I would feel disappointed, I'd wonder why he wasn't putting more effort into wooing me.

But it wasn't his fault. I mean, why would he think that I would want things different? I had been playing the role of the "leader" from the beginning of our relationship. And he was fine with it. He had been quite comfortable on the "let her do everything" plan. He would have assumed that I was an adult and was responsible for my own behavior, and that if I was acting like the "leader" in our relationship, it was because I liked it that way. If I suddenly wanted to switch to the follower's role and was upset when he didn't take the lead, it wasn't *his* fault; it was *mine*.

If I hadn't been in such an anxiety-fueled rush to move the relationship forward, if I'd backed off a little at the beginning and made space so I could, in effect, "listen" to his behavior, I might have found out in the first week or two of dating him that he was a guy who preferred being the "follower" in a relationship. And it would have saved me a lot of time and heartache.

This is not some kind of "game-playing" or "rule-based" dating strategy. It's not about hiding your interest or acting aloof, it's about leaving the space to attract the kind of relationship that you really want. If I let a guy "lead" the pace of our relationship, at least in the beginning, I get to see who he is. I get to see how interested he is in me. I may find out that he never calls again after the first date. Or I may find out that he's wishy-washy about making plans. As disappointing as really seeing who a guy is up front can be, wouldn't you rather know that stuff before you've become emotionally invested in the relationship?

Another downside to me being the "guy" or the leader in a relationship is the fact that I may turn off a man who *likes* to lead. A man who likes to court a woman—a man who likes to be the one to make the plans, do the calling, etc.—in the beginning of the relationship will likely be turned off by a woman who doesn't let him.

Or let's say I go out with a guy and we really hit it off and then the next day I call him up and ask him out for a second date. Maybe that guy was planning on calling me and I beat him to it. If so, I've just robbed myself of something special—the wonderful feeling of *him* calling for the second date. Just like the follower who insists on asking men to dance or doing all the leading, I might miss a trip to Paris and wind up in Bakersfield.

## FOUL WEATHER FRIENDS

Of course the problem with listening, *really* listening, is that sometimes you hear something you don't want to hear. You may find that the adorable new guy you just met is paying alimony to three ex-wives, has a prison record, and doesn't believe in monogamy. Or, if you're already involved in a relationship with someone and you start really actively listening to who they are, you may find out that the relationship isn't right for you. And this is true of friends as well as lovers.

As I've learned to become less interested in giving my opinion and have become more interested in simply listening, I've found that most of my friendships have deepened, but sadly, I've lost some too.

I have a friend who used to RSVP for parties I was having and then not only not show up, but not even call to apologize. It drove me crazy. I found it rude and disrespectful. When I confronted my friend about it, she apologized profusely and assured me that it would never happen again, but SHE KEPT DOING IT!

I really enjoyed this person's company, and had been friends with her for several years, but I thought that maybe I had to let this relationship go. But luckily I discussed it with another close friend before taking an action I would have later regretted. My friend said, "Well, maybe you can just think of the situation like this: This is my friend who I've known for several years, and who I love, and who is really bad about showing up to parties when she says she will."

I laughed at myself. My friend's comment gave me a whole new perspective. I realized that I had another option. I could just accept my friend for who she is. It's like that old saying "Do you want to be right? Or do you want to happy?" It's perfectly reasonable for me to be bugged when my friend doesn't show up. Or call to explain why. But you know what? I adore her. And I'm willing to accept this part of her. Just as I'm sure she accepts a lot about me that drives *her* crazy. So I'm not advocating cutting loose all relationships with friends who have faults. We all have them. God knows I do! It's just a matter of what faults you can live with and still be happy.

But there were some friends I just couldn't continue to have in my life. I realized at one point that I had a few, what I call "*foul* weather friends." These are friends who will only bond with you over their *pain*, never their joy. They love to gossip, they love to complain, they cast themselves as victims in life and only seem to be happy when you're lying down there in the gutter with them. And, I'm embarrassed to say, that at one point in my life I was one of them.

But after a few years of dancing and practicing the principles of L.O.V.E., I changed; I was happier, I felt more fulfilled. I started focusing on what I could *contribute* to life, rather than what I could *take* from it. And as a result, I started to feel pretty happy most of the time. My "foul weather friends" not only lost interest in me, but some of them seemed to downright resent me. These foul weather friends—or I guess what some people would call "frenemies"—are the ones who leave me feeling exhausted and beat up after I talk with them. These are the ones who like to minimize my successes and almost seem to rejoice in my failures. And after I let these relationships go, it felt like dropping weights off my shoulders.

As I changed, I lost some friendships. But I gained others. Now I have a great group of friends and we're right there for one another when the chips are down, but we're there for one another when the chips are *up* too.

Dancing taught me how to pause; how to be patient; how to really listen. It taught me how to not be in such a rush to get results—to pause, enjoy the ride, check out the scenery.

"Oh, he spun me into a turn here. I wouldn't have thought of that. How cool!" Or "Wow, he put a pause there, and it matches the music perfectly." I don't just listen to the music and move my body according to my own ideas but I get to experience the ad-

"*The* dancing's so different when I just really let him lead than when I'm thinking, 'What is he going to lead?' or 'Why is he leading that?' And I think I'm learning that in my relationship too—that listening, and doing what someone asks you to do is not negative, and it's not being submissive—it doesn't take anything away from me. When you're willing to listen you can create the most beautiful things."

—SHOSHANNA, TANGUERA

venture of exploring the moment through another person's creativity. So, rather than giving up something by surrendering the lead, whether it's for a few minutes or for a few hours, I'm, in fact, gaining something, my experience of life is enhanced.

And it's the same *off* the dance floor. When I listen actively to another human being my life expands, I get to experience the world through another person's eyes. If I keep interrupting you because I think I already know what you're going to say, or I'm only interested in what you're saying as a jumping-off point to announce my own ideas, then I may as well be dancing, or living, *alone.*

Always remember that listening is a gift for both of you. I have a friend who volunteers as a spiritual aide at a local hospice. Her job is to bring comfort to patients with chronic illnesses in their final days. She says that sometimes she prays with them, but mostly she just listens. She's just present with them. She's just, in her words, "an active witness." And she says that it's an incredibly powerful feeling—it feels like *love*.

# ACTIVE LISTENING EXERCISES

### EXERCISE I: LISTENING WITH YOUR ENTIRE BODY

I recently watched a TED talk in which a famous percussionist did a presentation on listening.* She is hearing-impaired, and when she applied to college to study music they turned her down, telling her that they didn't know how to teach her because she couldn't hear. She explained to them that they had the mistaken idea that listening was something you do only with your ears. She told them that true listening happens with your *whole body*—your hands, your skin, your eyes—all of you. So in this exercise I want you to practice listening with your whole body.

### VERSION ONE

The next time you are outside, notice the temperature. How does the temperature feel on your skin. If it's very cold, what does it feel like? Does it feel sharp? Painful? If it were a color, what color would it be? Now, what does the cold *smell* like? What does ice smell like?

---

* TED is a nonprofit organization that sponsors lectures and other events from people at the forefront of the fields of technology, entertainment, and design.

*continues*

Or maybe you're reading this in summer. What does the heat feel like on your skin? Burning? OK, if that burning feeling had a smell, what would it be?

There's no right or wrong for this exercise. You're playing, you're just exercising your femininity. If we decide for the sake of the ideas expressed in this book that femininity is subtle, let's play in the subtlety, let's use our strong feminine sensuality, let's develop, or for some of us even *rediscover* that sensuality. But this is not the sensuality of sexiness, it's the sensuality of deep or active listening. It's a listening that is done with your *whole* body.

### VERSION TWO

If there's some piece of music that you love and you're very familiar with, and you can take the time, go into a room by yourself, lie down, turn on the music, and close your eyes. Then try to listen to the individual instruments. Try to hear the bass, for example (or any instrument that you can easily separate from the others); try to listen to only *that* instrument. Now, make that sound a color. What color is it? What does that sound smell like? How does that instrument feel on your skin? Soft? Sharp?

## EXERCISE 2: REFLECTIVE LISTENING

You will need a partner for this exercise. You can use your boyfriend, or your husband, but it might be nice to find a girlfriend who's also working on this technique, so you can practice with someone you feel free to make mistakes with.

The following is a version of a classic therapeutic tool that is sometimes called "reflective listening."

Place two chairs in front of each other and sit so the two participants in the exercise—Partner A and Partner B—are facing each other.

Partner A shares something with Partner B.

It could be "I love french fries" or "I don't know if I'm in love with my husband anymore."

The level of what you share is for you to determine based on the level of intimacy you share with your partner. But since this exercise is really about learning to listen, and we won't be giving any feedback in this exercise, it might be best to keep the sharing on lighter or more superficial topics.

Partner A shares for up to three minutes, and Partner B listens very carefully. When it's clear that A has finished speaking, B takes a breath, then repeats back what A has said.

*continues*

It doesn't have to be word for word; it's not a memorization exercise but a deep or *active* listening exercise.

So B repeats or paraphrases what A has just said, saying something like: "I think what you're saying here is . . ." or "What I hear you saying is . . ."

When partner B repeats, she should try her best to make A *feel* heard. How? Again, make sure that when you're the one repeating, you don't just parrot your partner's words back to her with no opinion or emotion. If, for example, Partner A says with great enthusiasm, "I love my new tango shoes!" then Partner B doesn't *mimic* A's emotion, but *reflects* it. So B says, "I hear you saying that you LOVE your new tango shoes!" If B is really connected in a deep listening way to A, B will probably get excited about those shoes too.

Now B shares, and A repeats. Do this for a few rounds.

As with all the others in this book, do these exercises for as long and as often as you wish.

*chapter four*

"*There's* a woman who was a very successful television producer for many years who came to the studio once to check it out. She watched a class and she said, 'Never! I'll never let a man tell ME what to do on the dance floor.' And I thought, 'Well, OK, that's why you're the age you are and you're still single. Because you've always got to be in control, lady. And if you've got to be in control, it just isn't going to work.'"

—JULIE FRIEDGEN, OWNER,
THE TANGO ROOM DANCE CENTER

A t this point you're probably thinking to yourself, "OK, so you're telling me how great it is to 'follow,' and how wonderful it is to 'listen,' but what if my leader is a jerk? What if he wants to lead me right off a cliff! To 'follow' him would be just plain stupid!" And you're absolutely right. A leader has to *earn the right* for your follow. Remember, you're a *goddess*! Your leader must prove he is *worthy* of you.

While being led on the dance floor can be an utterly transcendent experience, sometimes it can be like dancing with a leering construction worker. There's nothing creepier than some greasy guy with body odor pressing his sweaty brow against your newly washed hair and perhaps even (egads!) whispering sweet nothings in your ear.

Or maybe some guy has taken five tango lessons and he wants to show you (and everyone else in the milonga) what a great dancer he is by doing every stupid, overly dramatic tango move you've ever seen—like drags across the floor, or, God forbid, a lift!

Allowing yourself to be manhandled in any way is not what

this book is about. In fact, it's the opposite. It's about literally stepping into your true feminine power. So if someone is hurting you, or behaving inappropriately, and after you let him know, he still doesn't change, you leave. Period. End of statement.

The very first time I dance with a new leader, I'm looking to find out if our combination feels right. I'm going to check out, for example, his height—"Oh, he's taller than me, is he *too* tall?" Or "He's shorter than me, is he *too* short?" Does our embrace feel comfortable? Do I like his smell? How is his touch? How does his arm feel on my back? Does it feel nice? Or is he holding me too tightly? Or too softly? As we begin to move, do I feel secure in his lead? Do I feel safe in his arms? Do I feel like he's communicating with me? Does his lead feel wonderful—like a gentle caress? Or is he roughly pushing and pulling me? Throwing me off my balance and poking his fingers into my back? Does he give me time to move, to make embellishments? Is he protecting me on the dance floor? Or is he dancing me right into other couples? Do we have chemistry? Are we compatible?

> "*Ginger Rogers did everything Fred Astaire did, but backwards and in high heels.*"
>
> —BOB THAVES, IN A *FRANK AND ERNEST* COMIC STRIP

Even if a guy is a great dancer, his style just may not be right for me. Maybe we don't hear the music the same way—maybe he moves too fast for me or too slow. In that case, I don't have to make either of us wrong. But I also don't have to force myself to dance with him. It's never healthy to twist myself into a pretzel trying to make something work if the partner isn't right for me—in dance or in life.

A follower (goddess) says no to a potential partner if she doesn't like the way he leads. If it doesn't feel good to be in his arms. If she's seen him dance with other women, and he's clumsy and un-protective of them on the dance floor. (Remember, most of the time the follower is dancing *backward*, so you need to know that your leader is looking out for you.)

Some leaders almost dance *at* you. It's like they're trying to make themselves look good by making you, their partner, look bad. Some make disparaging faces when you don't execute your moves in a way they approve of. Sound familiar? Like a man who puts you down in public, or criticizes your cooking, or the way you dress, or your body, or even the way you laugh!

Or perhaps a leader isn't trying to make you look bad, but he has only one way of dancing. And that's it, take it or leave it. He isn't interested in enjoying the way *you* move during the dance. He isn't interested in seeing what embellishments and leads make you smile—make you look and feel beautiful—which ones *you* like. This man doesn't want to be in relationship with you, he wants to use you as a prop so he can execute his moves. It's like making love. Do you want to make love with a man who only cares about his own pleasure, or a man who delights in yours?

# I SAY TOMATO AND YOU SAY,
# "YOU'RE TOO TALL FOR ME"

There's a guy I know from tango who's a great dancer and a great guy; he's someone I'm always happy to see when I go out dancing. He's been friendly to me from the very beginning. Because of my habit when I was first dancing of kicking my partners in the shins with my stilettos, he even has a nickname for me: "La Peligrosa Pelirrojo" (in English, "The Dangerous Redhead"). We have a great rapport together as people. But he *never* asks me to dance.

So one day I asked him, "Dario, you're always so nice to me, but how come you never ask me to dance?" He looked at me for a moment, and then said, "Peligrosa, come here for a moment." He pulled me over to a mirror and we stood side by side.

"*Mira,*" he said. (In English—"Look.")

Well, Dario is about five-four and I'm five-seven in bare feet. In my tango heels I'm five-eleven. He smiled and said, "*Comprendo?*"

I cracked up. Dario is an elegant and sensual dancer. When he goes to a milonga, he's always impeccably groomed and wears a perfectly tailored suit. The "look," the outward aesthetic of the dance, is very important to him. But because of our difference in height, when he dances with me, he doesn't look like the dashing tanguero of his dreams. He looks like my son.

Dario likes me very much as a person. But he just doesn't like the way we look together dancing. It's not personal. There's nothing wrong with either of us. We just don't make a good dance partnership. And you know what? Even though Dario rejects me as a partner, I don't feel the same way; I would dance with him anytime, anywhere. I ADORE dancing with him. He's a great leader. But he simply doesn't feel the same way about me. And as they say, "Them's the breaks."

And it's the same in dating. When you're dating someone new, you're getting to know each other—you're checking to see if the chemistry and compatibility are right.

If I date a guy for a few weeks or months and he doesn't end up wanting me as a life partner—a girlfriend, a wife, whatever— it doesn't mean there's anything wrong with him or me. The combination just doesn't work for one or both of us. I have so many girlfriends who, if a guy rejects them, they instantly find fault with *themselves*. It's often so hard for us women to remember that if a relationship doesn't work out, it's not necessarily because of something lacking in us. So many of my single girlfriends immediately think there's something wrong with them if a guy doesn't call for a second (or third or fourth) date.

"Oh, I revealed too much, I scared him away." "Oh, I should have dressed sexier." Blah, blah, blah.

## BEWARE OF "FEEDBACK"

Perhaps being an actress for so many years has helped me to have a thicker skin about all this. After an audition an actor sometimes receives feedback from the people she has auditioned for. Here's some of the feedback I have received in my thirty-plus-year career:

"She's not pretty enough."

"She's too pretty."

"She's not sexy enough."

"She's too sexy."

"She's too old."

"She's too young."

"She's too tall."

"She's too short."

You get the picture.

If I tried to change myself to align with everyone's idea of what I should be on any given day, I'd end up in a mental institution. Although a lot of actors dread the feedback that "they just went another way," it really is the most honest. If the powers-that-be don't think you're right for a certain role, it doesn't mean that you're not right in general, for all roles, in perpetuity! Someone once told me, if you're an orange, don't try to be an apple. You'll always be second rate. You might not make a good apple but you make a fantastic orange.

One of my first major acting roles was on a television series from the eighties called *Falcon Crest*. At the final audition, there were three actresses up for my part: Janine Turner (the gorgeous brunette from the nineties TV series *Northern Exposure*); the stunning blonde Heather Locklear; and red-haired, freckle-faced me.

Now, I'm certainly not more beautiful or talented than either of these actresses. *Please!* I feel lucky just to have been in the same category as them. But as luck would have it, that day the powers-that-be happened to be looking for an "orange." (Or in my case, a freckle-faced strawberry.)

*The cast of* Falcon Crest. *That's me as Vicky Gioberti in the second row, second from the left.*

It's not that feedback can't be helpful sometimes. It can be good to know that you need to improve your technique. Professionally if I do badly on an audition and it's because of something under my control—like a need to refine my comedy technique—it's helpful to know about it. In my personal life, if I hurt a friend's feelings or am unknowingly disrespectful in any way to my guy, I want to know.

On the dance floor I may be unaware of some way that I'm moving my body that's making things awkward or uncomfortable for my leader. But most of the time it's really not about skill, it's just about type, an ephemeral "something." My friend, talent manager Joan Sittenfield, explains it this way: "It's like when you go into Baskin-Robbins for ice cream, and that day you happen to be in the mood for butter pecan; strawberry doesn't commit suicide."

And always remember, on a date or on the dance floor, you're "auditioning" *him* too.

## DANCE A TANDA

Traditionally at a milonga, the tango music is played in sets called "tandas." A tanda is a collection of three to five songs, which are separated by a "cortina." Cortina means "curtain" in Spanish and is a one- to two-minute pause between tandas, where the dancers choose to stay together or use it as an opportunity to say, "Thank you," and have a rest or maybe even change partners.

(An important aside to anyone who is considering dancing the Argentine tango: at a traditional milonga, if you say, "Thank you," it's a polite euphemism for "I'm done dancing with you." So, if after the first song with your new leader you feel as if you were just whisked away to the terpsichorean equivalent of a multiple orgasm, do not, I repeat, do not breathlessly express your gratitude by saying thank you to your leader. He will assume you want him to walk you back to your seat. I can't tell you how many great leaders I caused to walk me off the dance floor prematurely by saying thank you after a *good dance*!)

In Los Angeles, when I was first learning to dance tango it was explained to me that unless the dance is completely horrific, it's very rude to dance just *one* song with a partner; you should always dance at least two. In Argentina, the custom is to dance a full tanda.

So when you say yes to dancing with a new partner, you are, in fact, making a commitment. Unless the leader is really crazy and hurting you or something, you'll stick it out for at least a couple of songs, or even a tanda. Then you decide if it's worth a second tanda, or a third, or maybe even decide that you want to spend the rest of the evening dancing with that same partner.

Sure, on the dance floor and in life, with some people you just *click*—within a few moments you feel as if you've known them your whole life. But even if you have chemistry with someone, you still need to go slow enough to find out if you're in fact *compatible.* For that reason, it's always best to dance (or date) a full tanda.

Sometimes it takes longer to get to know someone. Sometimes when you first dance with a new partner—or are first dating someone new—it takes time for that chemistry to kick in. This isn't necessarily a bad thing. Just because you don't have an instant

LEFT: *Me dancing with my dear friend and one of my first tango teachers, Moti Buchboot, at Divo Milonga in Santa Monica, CA.*

ABOVE: *My first trip to Buenos Aires in 2005—and dancing with my friend Victor Gilinsky at the famous Confitería Ideal.*

click with someone, it doesn't mean he isn't worth getting to know better. I've had some dance partners that were challenging to dance with at first—their leads were very subtle, their footwork was fast—but I never felt they were dancing *at* me, or deliberately trying to lead me astray. So I kept dancing with them whenever they asked me, because I knew that dancing with them would help me to become a better dancer.

So when you're dating, if the person is nice, I say to date at least three to five dates, a full tanda, before deciding whether or not he's right for you. Sometimes two people don't hit it off right away on the dance floor—or in life—but sometimes the most beautiful and lasting partnerships take a while to form.

> "*Let* go of the image, so you can see the vision."
>
> —HUBERT SELBY, JR.

As the writer Hubert Selby, Jr., so loosely pointed out, sometimes our image of what kind of person (or job, or lifestyle) is going to bring us happiness may not be as good as what we might receive if we were willing to let go of our preconceived ideas. I certainly found this with my guy.

When a friend offered to set me up on a blind date with a fellow actor, at first I told him he was out of his mind, that it'd be like trying to mate two peacocks. But at the time, I was getting a bit sick of being single. I was growing tired of kissing my neighbor's cat on New Year's Eve. So I decided to give it a shot.

And I'm so glad I did. Some of the things I love and appreciate the most about my guy are the same qualities that make him a good actor. He's sensitive, very funny, very comfortable openly expressing emotion, and extremely affectionate. My image of the kind of partner I needed in order to have a happy relationship wasn't as great as the vision that life had in store for me.

I have a girlfriend who was raised in a very loving and demonstrative Jewish family. They're from New York City and have a typically New York City style—funny and loud. At their family dinners, everyone argues and laughs and talks over one another, but they have lots of love.

My friend got set up on a date with a wonderful young man. He was handsome, intelligent, and sweet, had a great job, but grew up in a very different environment from my friend. He comes from a reserved Protestant family and was raised on the family farm in Iowa. While his family was just as full of love as my friend's, their style was very different. Their family dinners were quiet and polite.

My friend really liked this guy, but when they were having their first few dates she would call me saying she felt nervous around him because she couldn't "read" him. He made her nervous because his emotional style was so different than hers. I told her that since he sounded like such a nice guy, perhaps it was analogous to those times when I dance with an excellent leader but have trouble understanding his lead. Sometimes the answer isn't to change partners, but for me to have a more open mind. I may need to practice listening in a deeper way, to get out of my comfort zone.

I encouraged my friend to keep seeing this man. And as she got to know him better, she found that indeed sometimes still waters run deep. She grew to love his quiet personality. She has a very stressful job in the entertainment industry, and over time she found that his more gentle energy calmed her down. He was exactly the kind of person she needed in her life. And now they're engaged to be married. If my friend had been too quick to throw away the relationship because of chemistry, she might have missed out on the love of her life.

# BE THE GUY
# YOUR MOTHER ALWAYS
# WANTED YOU TO MARRY

Back when I was dating, the kind of person I was usually attracted to was what I called the nineteenth-century-consumptive-poet/ underfed-heroin-addict type. Think Bud Cort in that old movie from the seventies *Harold and Maude* (he was suicidal and pale— yum!) or Anthony Perkins in *Psycho*. Really. Guys like that made my heart sing. And if they happened to be in a band and had a fear of commitment, all the better. Why did I love these guys? The drama, baby! It was like I didn't really feel alive unless I was pining over some romantically challenged guy.

My friends kept trying to do dating interventions. They kept admonishing me to change my type. They kept telling me that I was "picking" the wrong kind of person.

So I would dutifully try to "pick" a different kind of person— I would try to force myself to be attracted to the "right" kind of guy. You know, someone without more tattoos than bare skin, or track marks, someone *nice*, but it never worked. When I tried to "pick" the right kind of guy, I felt bored.

And I met some really great guys! I still know some of them now, and many of them are married and have families, and it would have been wonderful if I had been able to somehow make myself fall in love with them. But the fact is, I wasn't ready for the kind of relationship I longed for. The problem wasn't that I was "picking" the wrong type; the problem was that *I* was the wrong type.

At one point I finally stopped looking outside myself for the solution. I gave up the idea that finding the right guy would solve all my relationship problems and instead took responsibility for who I was at the time. I didn't need to change my *type*; I needed to change *myself*. If I wanted to attract a different kind of guy, *I* needed to *be* different.

## PRACTICE MAKES PERFECT

When I began learning the tango, I spent many hours in dance class and practicing at home in an effort to become a better dancer. And as I improved, a whole new strata of partners opened up to me—the better leaders started to enjoy dancing with me. It wasn't that they didn't like me as a person before I spent time perfecting my dance skills, but in order to really have a good dance partnership with me, I needed to have a certain skill level to be able to interpret their lead. I had to put in my practice time.

It's like any sport. If you're a great tennis player, you might enjoy batting a ball around with a friend who's a beginner, but at some point you're going to want to be challenged. You're going to want to test your mettle with someone at your level, or even beyond. As they say, birds of a feather flock together. Or like attracts like. If you want to attract a better partner, first you have to *be* one.

# KEEP THE DRAMA IN THE DRAMA

A very wise person once told me that when we do things that are bad for us (like repeatedly attracting and staying in unhealthy relationships), there has to be some kind of payoff—there must be something we *love* about that situation or we wouldn't do it. So if we want to give up the behavior, we have to be willing to give up the payoff too.

That may sound crazy. I mean what could the payoff possibly be to a bad relationship? Interesting question.

I have a very close friend who, like me, was once involved with a guy who was very jealous. He would always accuse her of dressing provocatively, of flirting with other guys, and she wasn't. She was absolutely loyal to him. She was deeply in love with this man and had absolutely no interest in other guys.

In an effort to allay his fears, she started dressing in a way that minimized the assets of her figure. It was like she put on a virtual burka—she wore drab, shapeless clothes, she would keep her eyes cast down when they were out in public so that he wouldn't think she was trying to flirt with other guys. Sometimes her efforts would result in a temporary return of her boyfriend's affections, but he would always revert to his jealous ways, and usually even worse than before. So rather than helping things between them, my friend's efforts seem to have had the exact opposite effect. The more she tried to change herself, in an effort to make her man feel less threatened, the more jealous he became. It was like feeding a wild animal red meat: the more she fed his jealousy by trying to change herself to fix it, the stronger it became.

All of her friends, including myself, were concerned—we kept telling my friend to "leave the jerk"—I mean, it wasn't like she was dependent on him financially or there were children involved— she was free to leave anytime. But she wouldn't. She kept saying, she "loved him too much" to leave him. And she was certain that if she just kept at it, at some point he would see the light.

One day I took my friend out for some tea and a serious heart-to-heart. I suggested that we turn the situation with her boyfriend around and that we not look at her as the "victim" but as a willing participant. I suggested she ask herself, even if it didn't seem to make sense on the surface, what she might be getting out of her boyfriend's jealous behavior—what her payoff might be in this relationship. We hashed it out for a while and this is what came out: The situation was giving her a false sense of *control*. When her boyfriend felt jealous, he would "punish" her by withdrawing emotionally. Then she would try to get him to come back by suppressing her femininity. She had become addicted to the push and pull. It was exciting. And in some ways it made her feel strangely powerful.

She had the idea that altering her behavior could change her boyfriend. That she could somehow control his moods and his affection toward her—that she could make him love her by changing her personality.

Also, she was spending so much time in the drama of their relationship that it kept her really busy! So busy that she didn't have to take responsibility for her own creativity.

My friend was a screenwriter. A successful one. But during her relationship with this man, she had not written a thing.

So how were these things payoffs? Well, for one, my friend had grown up with an alcoholic parent. And in our talk that day she realized she was mimicking some of the behaviors she had learned as coping mechanisms as a child. Her mother would always tell her to keep quiet when her dad was drunk so she wouldn't "set him off." My friend was led to believe that she was somehow responsible for her dad's behavior. That if she could make herself small and quiet enough, she could somehow control her father's drinking. And that way he'd be a more loving father.

The other payoff was that she became so busy managing all the chaos in the drama of her relationship with her boyfriend that this provided her with a perfect excuse to avoid doing her work. As any writer or creative person knows, it's a lot easier to have a fight with your boyfriend than face the empty page. My acting teacher, Roy London, always used to say to me when I was a young actor, "Keep the drama in the drama"—meaning, don't create so much drama in your life that you have nothing left for the stage or screen.

All this "drama"—all this push-pull passion with her boy-friend—*seemed* like love, but it wasn't. Just as dancing with a leader shouldn't wrench your back or tweak your shoulder joint, real love shouldn't hurt.

After she figured out what her payoffs were, it was like an evil spell had been broken. My friend realized that the pain of the relationship was outweighing the payoffs. She left her boyfriend and is now happily married and writing again.

I did the same thing in *my* life. I realized that the payoff to the kind of guy I had been attracted to before my husband was mostly drama. There was always a lot of push-pull in my relationships with those consumptive poets and commitment-phobic musicians and artists. It felt exciting in some ways, but the "love" I experienced in these relationships was more like a feeling of longing and anxiety.

One day I decided that I wanted what my parents have. A partner. Someone you can count on. A best friend. Sure I had received some beautiful love poems and was mentioned in the liner notes of a few records, but a poem or a CD doesn't keep you warm at night. I wanted a life partner. Not someone I had to love from afar.

So rather than blaming the "type" of guys I was dating, I worked on myself. I went to therapy and discovered that my attraction to these kinds of guys stemmed from my own fear of commitment. That my payoff from the kind of relationships I had been having was actually that I spent a lot of time alone! But once I became willing to give up the payoff of keeping love at bay, a funny thing happened. When I changed, the men who I was attracted to changed.

I no longer found it sexy or attractive if a guy treated me badly, if he didn't call when he said he would, if he constantly needed space, if he was a selfish lover. As my self-esteem grew, I became attracted to a different kind of person. And it was effortless. Shortly afterward I met my guy.

I think the best way to find out whether a partner is right for you, in dance or in a relationship, is not to look at the two of you as individuals, but at what is created by your union. Is your dance beautiful or clumsy? Do people look at you with appreciation and admiration? Or do they look away? What is that third entity created by your union?

> "*When you have the right partner, it just makes it effortless. You just flow. There's no thinking, no concentrating, no, 'What am I going to do next?' You just move. And the music and the intimacy that the dance creates—that's when you fall in love with your partner, and when the music is over, it's over!*"
>
> —DAS, TANGUERA

In dance, even if the person is challenging to dance with, is it the kind of challenge that makes you dance better? Are you having fun? Do you feel appreciated?

In romantic relationships, ask yourself: How is your life going while you're in this union? With my old "type," my life got worse. I was unhappy. I was insecure and anxious most of the time. My outside life deteriorated—work, other relationships—because all my energy was being spent managing my romance.

And it works with platonic relationships too. Does this friend "get" you? Do you feel uplifted and understood? Seen? If not, why are you in it?

Check with your gut. How does this friendship or romance or dance partner make you feel? What does your *whole* life look like when you're in a particular relationship? Is your life better or worse as a result of this union? Are you more confident? Happy? Accomplishing more? Or are you diminished by this combination?

One of my acting students is a young woman in her twenties; she's been dating a guy for a few months who just doesn't treat her right. She asked me what I thought she should do about the relationship, and I told her that I wasn't qualified to give that kind of advice, that in matters of love you have to follow your own heart. I suggested she ask herself, if she had a daughter, would she want her to be with this guy? Would she want her own little girl to be in this relationship? She paused for a moment, and then said, "No, I wouldn't." And I said, "Well then, honey, why are you casting your pearls before swine?"

The words below are from one of my favorite leaders, Gabriel Kaplan. He is originally from Argentina (he's the one who "begged" me to dance in the Chapter Three: L Is for Listen) and he met his beautiful wife, Shoshanna, on the dance floor:

"As a leader, I follow. I suggest. I say, 'OK, we'll start this movement in this direction.' But different partners react in different ways. So when the leader suggests a direction, it's just a suggestion. You suggest a primary direction and then wait to see what happens—what she does—and then you follow *her*. And then the next step—again—you suggest, 'OK, let's go this way.' But each time, *she's* going to define exactly what your suggestion of 'move this way' means. So in this way it's a continuous communication. I might say, 'Let's go left.' But depending on the length of her stride, 'left' could be longer or shorter. Or 'left' could be a little bit more in front or more in back. So you're waiting for *her*, see? To see what *she* does, and then you follow that.

"So with Shoshanna, I might say, 'Let's go to Mammoth,' and she might say, 'Yes,' but I have no idea how exactly it's going to happen—what time we're going to leave, what the road is going to be like, what exactly we're going to be doing when we get there—we invent that together, the two of us."

## LEAD/FOLLOW EXERCISES

These exercises will give you a taste of what it's like to both lead and follow, even if you've never partner danced. You will need a partner for this exercise and a scarf, or other soft piece of cloth, to use as a blindfold.

### FOLLOW THE LEADER
#### VERSION ONE

Do this exercise in a room where there's enough space to move around a bit without crashing into anything (furniture, the family dog, etc.). And feel free to put on some music if you like, just make sure it has a slow tempo.

Face your partner and decide who is going to "lead" and who is going to "follow." The follower wears the blindfold.

Now grasp each other's forearms with the leader's arms on the bottom. Make sure to position yourselves so there's at least a foot or so between you to make it an "open" embrace.

Now the leader starts moving the follower around the room. The leader shouldn't try to "trick" the follower, but should be gentle and clear enough in his lead that the follower understands and feels safe.

The follower should just surrender. She should just do her best to "listen" to what her partner is saying.

Do this for five minutes or so, and then switch roles.

### VERSION TWO

Now do the same exercises without the blindfold and see if it feels different. Is it harder or easier to follow without the blindfold?

### VERSION THREE

Do the exercises again (with or without the blindfold) as someone from your Goddess List. Try to follow once as her. Try to lead once as her. Notice if you move differently.

Again, there is no right or wrong in this exercise. And feel free to play with this as often as you like.

*chapter five*

# O Is for
# Open Your *Heart*

*"Tango is so emotional—the music is always*
*telling an emotional story, usually a love story,*
*a story of love lost, so if you don't open*
*your heart to the pain that's in the music,*
*you can't express yourself through the dance."*

—NANCY, TANGUERA

In Argentine tango the position of the dancers' bodies is very different than in most other ballroom dances. The dancers incline toward each other. Chest forward. You lead with your heart. Perhaps this is why it's sometimes called "the dance of passion." The man (or leader) leads with his chest, and the follower, in effect, follows the leader's heart around. So I guess you could call tango dancing a meditation of the heart. And this meditation, this opening of the heart, sometimes causes people to change . . . into themselves.

*"You can close your eyes to the things you do not want to see, but you cannot close your heart to the things you do not want to feel."*

—UNKNOWN AUTHOR

I think that it was a kind of midlife crisis that led me to want to learn to dance the Argentine tango—my own special version of buying a candy-apple-red convertible.

That day in my scene-study class, when I saw my student dancing his sad solo tango, tracing those circles on the floor with his feet, it spoke to something in my heart. It's like when you hear a certain piece of music and you're surprised to feel tears forming in your eyes and an ache in your chest. You didn't even realize you felt sad, but something in the melody is giving some unspoken part of you a voice. My student's movements in class that day were telling the story of the broken heart I didn't know I had.

At that time in my life I was at a crossroads. I had been a professional actress since I was a child. I'd had a respectable career—had made a living, had even had a taste of celebrity. But as I'd gotten older, the roles had become fewer and less interesting. I was pretty much only getting offers to play distraught mothers, over-the-hill socialites, and dare I say it? "Cougars." Working myself up to cry for every audition was getting exhausting, my beige cashmere twin set was getting a little threadbare, and I was sick of making fun of the fact that I was still attractive and sexually alive at the by-Hollywood-standards ripe old age of forty-five.

I had recently begun teaching acting, and even though I loved it, and found it very fulfilling, I missed having a forum for my own creativity. I had a great boyfriend, but the truth was I wasn't satisfied with our relationship. I wanted a deeper commitment. I wanted us to get married. But even after five years of living together, my guy still "wasn't ready."

Sometimes I considered moving out, but I had so many girlfriends my age and older who were single and longing for a relationship that I was afraid of losing what I had. I kept telling myself that since we didn't have kids, marriage wasn't important, that "it's just a piece of paper." I was lying to myself.

*"I was dancing with a man and it was amazing, and I realized it was time to go, and he said, 'Well, I'll see you here tomorrow . . .' and I said, 'Oh, I can't come tomorrow,' and we kept dancing. Then he asked me again, and I said I really can't, and he said, 'Well, what could be more important than dancing the tango?' And we're in this close embrace and we've been together now for several hours, you know, dancing very close, very intimate, the most intimate I've been with a man other than my husband in fifteen years. And he says again, 'What could be more important than dancing the tango with me tomorrow?' I stopped, and I pulled away from him just slightly, and I said, 'Asking my husband for a divorce.'"*

—CAROLYN, TANGUERA

As I got to know other women in the dance community, I found I was not alone in my feeling that something was missing in my life. I was struck by how many women had just recently experienced the breakup of a long-term relationship or were considering a major career change, facing a serious health issue, or were at some other kind of important crossroads in their lives. When they began dancing, they changed. As their bodies opened, it was like their hearts and minds opened as well.

And if they were trying to push down issues—certain truths in their lives—all those issues came bubbling up to the surface. For some of them it meant making drastic changes in their lives. For some it meant leaving their relationships. For some it meant finding a new lease on life and finding love on the dance floor. And for some it meant a sexy rejuvenation of the great relationships they already enjoyed.

> *"Go to your bosom; knock there, and ask your heart what it doth know."*
>
> —WILLIAM SHAKESPEARE

Tango changed Julie Friedgen's life. A professional screenwriter, she now owns the Tango Room dance center and co-hosts the El Encuentro milonga with her life partner, Angel:

"It was shortly after my fiftieth birthday and my husband and I had a big, beautiful sixty-two-hundred-square-foot home, with a backyard with a waterfall and a koi pond. And I was wandering through my house, thinking, 'Why do I have this hole in my heart and in my soul?' Well, you know that saying, 'Be careful what you wish for?' I wished for passion. I said to myself, 'Before I die I want to feel turned on. I want to make out with somebody. I want to feel like a teenager. I want to be excited. I want to *feel* something.'

"Now, my husband was a very nice man, a very, very sweet man. The perfect husband. Except, there just was no spark there. So, I threw that wish, or prayer or whatever you want to call it, out to the universe or to God or to whoever is out there—that I wanted passion in my life. Well, that was in April of ninety-six. I took my first tango lesson in June of ninety-six.

"I started taking dance lessons and attending the milongas at the Argentine Association in Burbank. And there was this man there named Angel. He was really loud and gregarious and would go around kissing all the women and I remember thinking, 'Oh, what a jerk!' Well, it wasn't in my plans. I mean, if one night at that milonga my fairy godmother sat on my shoulder and said to me, 'Julie, you are going to leave your husband for one of the men in this room,' Angel is the last person I would have chosen! He was the class clown! The loud guy, the obnoxious guy—if there's a commotion, you know he's at the center of it! And you guessed it. I fell in love with him.

"He's so in love with life, so in love with 'the moment'—when he's mad he's one hundred percent mad, when he's happy he's one hundred percent happy, when he's hungry he's one hundred per-cent hungry, when he's horny he's one hundred percent horny! There's no in-between with him, so his energy creates this life force!

"Well, one day, I asked myself the question, 'Who can I live without? Can I live without my husband, can I live without this big house on the hill, or can I live without this loud fat Argen-tine? And the answer was, I couldn't imagine the rest of my life without Angel. I just couldn't. And I still can't. And we fight like cats and dogs! But, it's the first time that I truly did what I wanted to do. I really followed my heart.

"Angel and I have been together twelve years now and I have not been bored for one second. Furious, yes. Annoyed, constantly. Enchanted at the most unexpected moments. But, bored, never. So, I would tell other women, 'Listen to that voice that comes from your heart. All the bad decisions I've ever made in my life were because I did not listen to that voice.'"

> *"There are things that we never want to let go of, people we never want to leave behind. But keep in mind that letting go isn't the end of the world, it's the beginning of a new life."*
>
> —UNKNOWN AUTHOR

Das Silverman also came to tango at a pivotal time in her life. After almost fifty happy years of marriage, her husband died of Parkinson's disease. With him gone, she felt lost and alone. That all changed when she began partner dancing.

"The first dance I remember learning was the Charleston, when I was five. Some of the bigger girls taught me. And then, when we were ten or twelve, and too young to go to the dances and have boyfriends, we would put the radio on. And every Monday night, Wayne King, the Waltz King, would have his show and we would dance to it, for a solid half hour. And then later, some of the big bands were coming in, like Benny Goodman, the Dorsey Brothers, and I met my husband. He was a musician. A drummer. And he would play the Palomar, and the Palladium, and when he played, I danced. He was on the bandstand, and I was on the dance floor dancing mambo!

"And we danced *together* too. We were firm believers in taking lessons. You don't just go out there and make a fool of yourself! So we were at Club Sarape one night, and there was this couple. It was the kind of scene where everybody made a circle; nobody danced, so they could watch this couple, Gino and Suzanne. And after they performed we asked them if they would teach us. And every Tuesday we would go and have our lesson. And at that time we were dancing a lot. This was in the late forties, early fifties. We used to drop our kids off at the movies—double bill—and then go to the Tea Dance at Ciro's. We just loved to go out and dance. And then, well, this is many years later now, he got Parkinson's. And I stayed at home with him. For eighteen years.

"So when he'd been gone about a year, I think, I was in my early seventies, a widow, and I just, well, I was at a low point. And one day, I went to the bakery to buy some bread, and I was walking back to my car, and I saw Arthur Murray's Dance Studio. And well, I wasn't doing anything at the time, and I thought, 'Dance, that sounds like fun, I'm going to go find out about it.' And I walked upstairs (with the bread) and I got to talking to the salesman, and he asked me if I'd ever had dance lessons, and I said, 'Yes, I had a teacher, his name was Gino Revelle.' And it turns out that Gino's daughter, Lucia, worked there! So of course I immediately signed up! And they used to have these little socials for the students, and I met some lovely people. If you can imagine what that was like—I'd just spent eighteen years with a husband with advanced Parkinson's. To suddenly get out in the world, get dressed, to be in a social setting, with music, I just . . . there's no end to what dancing has meant in my life.

"Then, twelve years ago, I met Bill. I remember it was at Club

Pasión. And every Tuesday was tango night. I was there having dinner. I was sitting out a dance and he came over. He was wearing a navy blue blazer and white flannel slacks. You couldn't miss him. And he came over and asked me to dance, and they were playing swing, and I said, 'No, thank you, I don't do swing and I don't do turns.' And he said, 'Oh come on, give it a try,' and he gave me his hand. And I have NEVER let go! I know something good when I see it! I mean the way he led me, and the way he danced? I was not letting *that* go. That was two weeks before my eightieth birthday."

---

"*Wherever your heart is, that is where you'll find your treasure.*"

—PAULO COELHO

---

Susan Cousins, late fifties, was at the brink of divorce. She'd been with her husband thirty years, they'd raised two beautiful kids. But while their love for each other was strong, it was like that of a brother and a sister, rather than lovers. Dancing tango brought passion back to her marriage:

"My husband is my best friend. But we had zero sex life. At one point I think it was almost two years without . . . anything. We had so much affection, lots of cuddling, we love to 'spoon' when we sleep, but just no, you know . . . passion. It got to the point where I felt embarrassed even at the thought of having sex with him—it was like he was my brother or something, it just felt . . . wrong.

"But then one day a girlfriend of mine suggested I join her at a tango class. I didn't want to go . . . I've always had two left feet. I've been athletic all my life but I've always been a terrible dancer! But I thought, 'Oh what the heck,' and I went. Well, I don't know what happened, but I loved it! And before you know it, I was just kind of addicted. And I love the clothes, and those shoes! And then, well, something happened. One night I came home from tango class, and I just went right upstairs and woke my husband up, and . . . let's just say he doesn't feel like my brother anymore!"

> "*Before I met my husband, I'd never fallen in love, though I'd stepped in it a few times.*"
>
> —RITA RUDNER

Shannon Wilcox remarried a few years ago. Her husband doesn't dance, but he knows that it's an important part of what makes her the woman he fell in love with:

"A marriage isn't safe and strong and trustworthy, if one is afraid of letting someone express something that they love. I mean, my sweet husband, I said no to him so many times, and he finally said, 'Marry me, it would make me so happy!' And I said, 'I'm supposed to marry you because it would make YOU happy?' And then, something clicked, and he *got* it, he *got* me, and he said, 'Marry me, and sign a prenup that you will dance three nights a week. Or I won't marry you. Because if you're not happy, I'm not happy.' And of course I said yes.

"And now he'll say to me, 'Isn't it Saturday? Shouldn't you be getting on some spike heels and fancy pants?' I mean, he has never retracted the feeling behind that statement, that I had to dance three nights a week because it makes me so happy, because it's who I am. And consequently, he gets more from me; I dance two nights a week instead of three! And, if I'm lucky enough to feel it dancing, I bring home that sensuality, I take it home to my husband."

*"Surrender isn't throwing in the towel, it's releasing yourself into the arms of another."*

—DR. NICKI MONTI

Becka Fabian is an Iranian-born tanguera in her early fifties. Married with four kids by age thirty, she found her own separate identity as a woman on the dance floor. She and her husband, Caro, now host tango tours to Buenos Aires through their company, Becka Tango Tours:

"I was born and raised in an Armenian family, and Armenians are very traditional. Armenian women are known to be extremely caring mothers and that's how my mother was. And she taught me to be the same. For as long as I can remember, I've been a caregiver. And I've done it lovingly; it was never something I felt forced to do—I mean, my mother was the same, my sister was the same—so it's just how I was raised. And then I met my husband and we had two children right away—by age twenty I had two children. And then by twenty-nine I had four! So there were lots of things I couldn't do when I was younger like other people. I mean, at twenty I wanted to go dancing like other people my age, but I couldn't, I was changing diapers nonstop!

"My parents were both poets and I saw them dance tango back

in Iran, and they were just so, I mean, this dance is already poetic and if somebody dances it who also understands poetry . . . it was just so magical, so awesome to watch. And I had always wanted to learn it. But then I got too busy with raising my family, and I simply didn't have the time, so it came much, much later—in my early forties—after my children were grown.

"And it was the best! It came as an escape for me—to be able to escape the problems that I had. My daughter was in Iraq, serving, and my mother was chronically sick—she was not able to walk—and it was such a difficult time. And tango was a time for me to escape, a time just for me.

"So all my life I'd been caring and nurturing and nourishing, and that's a huge part of who I am but I had no personal identity. I didn't know who *I* was. I mean, I was my children's mother, I was my husband's wife, and I realized after tango, that all my friends had been my husband's friends! When I started dancing tango, I created my own friendships. And now, the connections that I have with my dance buddies—I don't want to lose that for anything!

"My husband started dancing tango about six months after I did. And then we bought an apartment in Buenos Aires. And it was kind of 'my thing,' so I started working on it. And I had to spend a lot of time being there by myself and, well, being alone; it was, oh my God, it was a different world! I had never done that in my life! I never knew what it was like to wake up and not have to worry about someone else. And I loved it! I loved the idea of just sitting in front of my computer with my pj's on and just listening to music, for *three hours* and having breakfast . . . I had never done that! Never had the chance, or the opportunity. So when I had this, it was like OH MY GOD! How come I have never done this? And I enjoyed it so much!

"So when I started dancing tango I felt like I was not only a wife, I was not only a daughter, I was not only my children's mother. I was, finally, *myself.*

"Now, I have to tell you that I used to be so shy—I can't tell you how shy I was. And with tango, I've totally grown up. I've become the woman that I am now. And I got so confident! And then, for a while, it was really difficult to take another lead! I was, like, 'What do you mean? I have to follow? I've done that my whole life!' It was almost insulting!

"But to be honest with you, when I really started to understand the idea of 'Just don't do anything—don't even think! Just give yourself to the leader. Just relax,' I discovered that following is not as bad as I thought it was! And of course, when you dance with a leader who knows what he's doing, it's like heaven! And it dawned on me, that in my life, a lot of times, if I had not followed my husband's lead, I may not have done the right thing. And that is something I'm very appreciative of. My husband is a sweetheart. He is a wonderful man and I honestly could not imagine being without him. I wouldn't be who I am in my life without him. He gives me the love on a constant basis that makes me the queen that I now feel I am."

> "*I* was once afraid of people saying, 'Who does she think she is?' Now I have the courage to stand and say, 'This is who I am.'"
>
> —OPRAH WINFREY

Reta Rose grew up an "army brat." Like the sergeant major he was, her father ruled over their family with an iron fist. Dancing was her ticket to a new life. (Reta also happens to be my mother.)

"When I was around five or six years old, I saw Rita Hayworth dancing in a movie. I remember it was in color, 'Technicolor,' they called it, and she was a redhead like me and since my first name was Reta, I decided that I was going to *be* her. I would dance anywhere I could, in the living room, on the lawn, and I didn't necessarily need to have an audience. I would just kick up my legs and fluff my skirt and carry on—that's my earliest memory of dancing. At that time I lived in a little town of about fifteen hundred people called Lehi, Utah, and we got traveling dance teachers from time to time, so occasionally I'd have a class. I was an 'army brat' so we would move around all the time to different states. My first formal training that I remember was in Lawton, Oklahoma, when I was around nine. The teacher's name was Jack Story. He taught an hour-long class of ballet and tap and stretching and I just took to it like a duck to water. And because my parents couldn't always afford lessons, I ended up cleaning— sweeping up the room and picking up clothes—to pay for my lessons, but this is when I knew what I wanted to do.

"Then, when I was seventeen, we were living in Cheyenne, Wyoming, and I was going to school and working as a waitress at the Jolly Ranger, making fifteen dollars a week. I used the money to pay for my dance lessons and clothes and things, and since there were five of us kids then, I gave my parents some money too to help with my room and board. And well, I lived in a very patriarchal-type home—what my father said *went*. It was a home where children were to be seen and not heard—personal expression and noise were *not* allowed. I don't want to go too much into details, but it was just very confining, and I guess nowadays you might call it abusive. And . . . I just knew that I needed to get out of that situation. And dancing became my ticket out of a life I needed to change.

"I had saved up to go to a dance convention in Los Angeles at the Sherry Biltmore Hotel. It was in August of 1955, when I was seventeen, right before I was going into my senior year of high school, and they brought in some professionals who gave us an audition, you know, just for fun, and to sort of impress us. And there was a tap choreographer there named Louis DePron—he was Donald O'Connor's choreographer—and I, along with some of the other girls, auditioned for him.

"Then, a few months later, as I said, I was having a lot of problems in my home situation, I got a telegram—would you believe—saying, 'We would like to use you for *The Donald O'Connor Show.*' *What!* I thought, *me?*

"It was December and I was a senior in high school and I went to my parents and said, 'I got this telegram with this offer and I would like your permission, but either way I'm going to go.' And that didn't sit too well—I was underage and I hadn't yet gotten my high school diploma. And my parents, they were always the ones that told me what I *could* do and *couldn't* do. They didn't like the fact that I said I was going one way or the other, but my father said, 'If you can get your high school diploma, *maybe* we'll allow it.' So I went to the dean of girls—I'd been a very good student, was up on all my grades—and she discussed the situation with the principal, and they said if you can pass the final regents exam you'll get your diploma. When do you want to take the test?

And I said, 'Tomorrow.' And they said, we can arrange it in about two days, and they did and I passed so I was guaranteed my diploma. So I went back to my father and I said that I would be graduating so therefore I can go, and he said, 'How are you going to afford it?' And I said, 'Well, I was hoping that maybe you could loan me the money.' And he said, 'No, if you want to go you're going to have to figure it out.' And then my brother Terry, who is one year older, and who understood the situation, went down to his room and came back and gave me a hundred and ten dollars, which you have to understand, a hundred and ten dollars at that time was like six or seven hundred dollars now—and he said, 'Now you've got the money.' My brother Terry was a boy of few words, but he really observed a lot. So anyway, that's how I left. That was in December, and we opened on the day after Christmas at the Sahara Hotel in Las Vegas. I was one of the two girls that were flanking Donald O'Connor and that was the start of my professional dancing career.

"But I'll tell you, even after I had children and I stopped dancing professionally, I found that it had given me something that I carried in all the other areas of my life. It gave me something that I had never had in my home life growing up as a kid: It gave me a feeling that I was worth something. I was really good at it and it gave me a feeling of 'Yes, I can do this. Yes I am somebody.'

"Then around ten or fifteen years ago, I had pretty much retired from working and I heard about the *Palm Springs Follies,* which as you know is a very popular variety show in Palm Springs featuring dancers age fifty and up. And I thought to myself, 'Gee, I wonder if I can still do that?' I mean, my mind said I could, but I wondered if my *body* still could. But then I thought, 'I'm going to try!' And I'll tell you something, it wasn't easy. I auditioned five

times before I got it! And I loved it. I was very proud to be in the show, especially since I'd worked so hard for it. But then, it was so all-encompassing. I had to live down in Palm Springs and I missed celebrating the holidays with my kids, and my grandkids, and I remembered why I'd given up dancing in the first place— my family was more important to me. So I stopped.

"And I'll tell you one more thing, the dancing I did in shows is not that different from partner dancing, because the choreographer sets the routine and basically 'leads' you, and you are basically the follower and the interpreter. And when you get a choreographer and a dancer who understand each other and jell, it's magic! Once in a while you have that combination that brings out the best in both of you and it's just enchanting! And how I feel about partner dancing is very similar: Once in a while you dance with someone and it's not even a matter of who's leading or who's following, but it's magic! And that's what I felt the first time I danced with your dad. He looked at me and said, 'You're the only one that's ever been able to follow me!' And I said, 'Really? Because I love the way you lead!'"

## IT'S OK TO WEAR YOUR HEART ON YOUR SLEEVE

Before I met my husband, I was often told by guys I dated that I was too "needy." It seemed I always picked guys who would

*My mom, Reta Rose, January 5, 1956, three days shy of her eighteenth birthday. Her first professional dancing job was as one of two girls in Donald O'Connor's Las Vegas club act.*

come on very strong and romantic and then after a while—a few months, weeks, or sometimes even days—they would start to pull away. Then, even if I wasn't that interested in them at that point, it would trigger me. And I would start to feel a kind of low-grade anxiety. "Uh oh," I would think, "there it is, my dreaded *neediness!*"

I always went right to the idea that the problem was in me, not the guy who was pulling away. I had the mistaken idea that my longing for emotional reassurance was not only wrong, but somehow bad.

In the first month or so of dating my guy, we were at the point where we were talking on the phone every day. So one day, I called him first thing in the morning and he wasn't there. Hmmm. Weird. But I left a message saying hello and to call me back. A few hours passed, and I didn't hear from him. So, I thought, "OK, he's busy, just calm down. He'll call."

So now, it's like five P.M., and I haven't heard from him. So I call him again. And I leave a voice mail (trying to sound very casual), "Hi there, just wondering what's happening. Give me a call. Bye!"

And now I feel the acute anxiousness start to kick in. Oh no! The dreaded NEEDINESS! Now it's six P.M. Where the hell is he? So, I call *again*. "Um, we had talked about having dinner tonight? Um, call me as soon as you get this!"

And now, I'm basically watching the clock. I putter around

*Me with my mom (sixty-seven years young) after a show.*
*She's in her costume as a "Long-Legged Lovely" with the*
Palm Springs Follies.

my house. I organize my sock drawer, la la la . . . Now it's six-thirty! Now it's seven! Seven-forty-five!

I am starting to lose it. It's happening again! Another guy is pulling away! Abandoning me! I knew it! I'm never going to have a relationship! I'll never find love! I'm doomed to dance alone through this world!

It's eight P.M. I call again. And, oh yes, this time I'm *crying*. Sexy, right? Alluring. Enigmatic. "Why"—sniff—"haven't you called? I'm"—sniff, snort—"waiting for you to call." Sob. "Call me"—sob, snort, sniff, sob—"please . . . !"

OK, at this point I'll save you the pathetic details, but let me just say that IT GETS WORSE FROM HERE! I call him every fifteen minutes for the rest of the night. And oh yes, this goes on for the entire night. I'm freaking out. I'm a mess. A big fat snorting loser. I have written copious self-pitying entries into my journal. I've called every girlfriend who will pick up the phone. I finally pass out at about three A.M. At around six-thirty A.M. I'm awakened by the ringing phone.

"HELLO?" I practically scream into the receiver. It's my guy.

"It's me! What's wrong? Are you OK?"

"Yes"—sob, cry, sob—"but why haven't you called me?"Sob sob sob.

"Honey, don't you remember? I was golfing. I was on the golf trip I told you about."

And then I remembered. Oh my God, he did tell me. He had told me the date a week or so before. And I forgot. Oh my God. He is going to be *so* outta here.

"Well, but, um"—sniff, sniff—"why didn't you remind me?"

"I . . . I don't know, I just thought . . . are you OK? Why are you crying?"

And I thought, oh great. Now I've really blown it. I am a frigging idiot. Here is this nice guy, this GREAT guy, and I have just completely ruined it with my frigging NEEDINESS! Now he'll disappear for sure. Oh hell, I may as well be honest.

"Because"—sniff—"I thought you were"—SOB!—"ABANDONING ME!" SOB, SNORT, SNIFF, SOB, SOB, REALLY BIG SNORT.

I prepare myself for his reaction. Ready myself for the all-too-familiar *cold and distant* sound to appear in his voice. The sound that says, "You're too needy. You are a desperate loser. You are freaking me out and I AM SO OUTTA HERE!" At that point I am certain that I will never hear from him again. But he surprises me.

"Oh sweetheart," he says in the most gentle and loving voice. "Do you want me to come over?"

And with that, my life changed. I felt my neediness fly out of my chest like a bird that had been trapped and flinging itself against the hard walls in a house when it finally finds an open window. I heaved a huge sigh, my whole body relaxed. And I knew right then, that with this man, it was OK to open my heart.

*"There's no left without right, no good without bad, no pleasure without pain, no happiness without sadness. And even though life can sometimes be painful, the only way to really feel joy is to live with an open heart. And the best way to open your heart is to fill it with so much gratitude that it overflows."*

—MICHAEL LALLY, POET

There's a guy who sometimes attends a certain Los Angeles milonga who's known as Crazy Billy. He's probably around seventy years old, is very thin, wears a black toupee that is a little too large for his head, has a shoe-polish black handlebar mustache, and always wears the same worn brown double-breasted suit that smells like a combination of Old Spice and dust. He lists a little to the left when he walks, and looks like he might tip over any minute. Usually, the only women who will dance with Crazy Billy are the newbies, because they don't know any better.

When I was in my first months of tango dancing and eager to learn, I used to dance with anyone who asked me. So one night Crazy Billy (although I didn't know his name at the time) appeared at my usual Saturday evening milonga, and after paying his entrance fee made his way jauntily around the room looking for a dance partner. I noticed that all the women he approached kind of averted their eyes or suddenly pretended to be deep in conversation, but I didn't think too much of it, I was there to dance!

So when Crazy Billy came around to my side of the room and asked me to dance, I said yes. As we stood together on the dance floor waiting for the first strains of the music, I got a taste of what I was in for. His toupee was slightly crooked on his head and was kind of dipping down toward his left eyebrow, his eyes were wide and a little mad looking through his thick aviator-style bifocals, as he smiled broadly and said: "I adore your gown! Did you design it?"

I was wearing pants. But they were long and slightly flowing so I thought, "Well, OK, it's an easy mistake, I'll give him the benefit of the doubt."

"Thank you," I replied.

Then the music started. He seized me in a tight embrace, clicked his heels together twice, and then swept us forward so strongly I was afraid we'd fall over. It was then I realized that this guy had absolutely no idea what he was doing. I'm not sure what he was dancing, but it wasn't the Argentine tango. It was kind of a waltzy, Hollywood-musical inspired, ballroomesque improvisation. And as he danced me around the floor, it was like Crazy Billy was in his own world, like he was living in an old movie— like in his mind I was a glamorous and floaty Ginger Rogers to his dapper and debonair Fred Astaire.

I glanced around the room as he twirled me and saw the regulars at the milonga looking at me and tittering with amusement. I felt like such a dope to have made the mistake of dancing with this nutty guy.

When the song was finally over, I said a hurried thank-you to Billy and quickly returned to my table. The more experienced tangueras laughed good-naturedly and said, "Oh my God! You should have seen your face! I can't believe you danced with Crazy Billy! We should have warned you!"

After that experience I always avoided Crazy Billy's glance when he made his rounds at the milonga, searching for a partner.

A few months after that, I was at the very same milonga and one of my favorite female tango dancers, Elizabeth Tambasco, walked in. She is an elegant and beautiful woman of around forty and a very accomplished dancer. I admire her greatly.

Elizabeth took a seat by the dance floor, and then, suddenly, Crazy Billy appeared out of nowhere and made a beeline for her. I realized that he was going to approach her and ask for a dance! I winced inside with embarrassment for him, certain he was going to be soundly rejected. But, to my surprise, Elizabeth said yes!

And as Crazy Billy whirled her unsteadily around the dance floor, Elizabeth looked as if she was having the time of her life. She smiled at him the entire time, looking into his face with such an expression of appreciation and joy, it was as if she *was,* in fact, dancing with Fred Astaire.

When the dance was over, Billy took Elizabeth's arm and proudly walked her back to her table. He pulled out her chair for her, bowed, gallantly kissed her hand, and said, with a perfect French accent, "*Merci, madame.*" Then, with a spring in his step, and beaming with happiness, Crazy Billy disappeared into the crowded milonga.

Since that night, whenever Billy asks me to dance, I always say yes.

*"A joyful heart is the inevitable result of a heart burning with love."*

—MOTHER TERESA

Of course I'd been aware of and have always tried to practice this concept, but dancing with Billy that night once again reminded me how important it is to do small kindnesses for other human beings whenever possible. And, of course, these small acts always bring much more to my life than they probably do to theirs.

In the same way, I make it a practice to do small acts of love for my guy, especially if I'm feeling mad at him. Things that he may not even notice. For instance, if I'm making dinner, I might try to arrange the food attractively on his plate instead of just slopping it on there as I usually do. Or maybe I'll wear my hair the way he likes, or put on a certain dress or blouse that I know he thinks is pretty on me. I love to read, but my guy likes to watch movies, so maybe I'll suggest we spend our evening in front of the flat screen instead of retreating to bed early to curl up with my book. Or maybe I'll simply suggest we both go to bed early . . . wink, wink. The point is for me to be proactive about expressing the love I have for my guy by turning it into action.

## TEA FOR TWO

My friend Dr. Nicki Monti shared with me an anecdote from her own life that I think exemplifies the idea of expressing love as an action.

At one point a few years ago, she would come home from a long day at work and her husband (who's retired) would say, "Hey, honey, would you make me some tea?"

And immediately everything in her would say, "WHAT? MAKE YOU SOME TEA? ARE YOU NUTS?"

She'd been working all day—being there for her patients, listening to their stories, giving them every drop of her attention. She'd been discussing loss, and heartbreak, and sometimes even suicide, and after all that, she thought, "Now you want me to bring my exhausted body into the kitchen and make you tea? While you've had the luxury of being home all day? You can make your own tea!"

And she said she had this voice screaming inside of her saying, "Don't you understand how tired I am? How exhausted? How overwhelmed? SCREW TEA!"

But then one day, she calmed down, and she realized that her husband's request wasn't about tea, it was about attention. Her husband had been feeling lonely—he'd been feeling like she was giving everything to everybody *except* him. He missed her. He felt unimportant in the scheme of her life. She said, "My dear supposed-to-be-my-priority husband wants to know that I care—really deeply care—about him. He wants to feel attended to."

So, for several days in a row, she came home and said, "Honey, how about I make you some tea?" She proactively offered it to him—what he needed—and you know what? After about three days, "He didn't need the tea."

---

## EXERCISES
## TO OPEN YOUR HEART

---

### EXERCISE 1: LISTEN WITH YOUR HEART

Pick five of your favorite songs or pieces of music. Try to pick five very different ones. My first list might include: Don McLean's "American Pie," Lady Gaga's "Let's Dance," Joaquin Rodrigo's "Concierto de Aranjuez," Louis Prima's "Sing, Sing, Sing," and Luciano Pavarotti singing the aria "Nessun Dorma" from Puccini's *Turandot.*

Once you've compiled your own list, like you did in the listening exercise in Chapter Three, find a quiet place where you can lay down, turn on the music, and close your eyes.

Play one of the songs and as you listen to it, try to listen not just with your ears, but with all your senses, and especially with your heart. This means to allow yourself to have an emotional connection with each piece of music and see what memories or feelings it evokes.

For example, I have very strong feelings of nostalgia connected to the song "American Pie." It reminds me of summer in the San Fernando Valley. Hot and dry, of course, but also with that great feeling of excitement and freedom when there's no school and each day is ripe with possibility.

*continues*

The summer I was thirteen years old, I took the bus to the record store with my little brother, Steve. When we got to the store, my brother bought me that record as a gift.

Whenever I hear the song, I feel very connected to how much I loved my little brother. And still do. And how much I treasure the shared memories of our youth. And how very sweet it was of him to buy me that record.

I can also remember purposefully studying the liner notes so I could memorize all the lyrics—something I used to do with every song I liked when I was that age. And I still remember every word of "American Pie":

*"A long, long time ago, I can still remember, how that music used to make me smile . . ."*

Do this exercise with each song on your list. If you like you can write down some of your memories in your journal.

The purpose of this exercise is simply to notice how listening to a song you love can open up your heart.

## EXERCISE 2: GRATITUDE LIST

### VERSION ONE

Quick, think of five things in your life you're grateful for!

*Here's my list:*

1. I can type
2. I can see
3. I love my husband
4. My parents are still alive
5. I can dance

Make doing a Gratitude List a game you play several times a day for the rest of your life. If you do, I guarantee your life will improve. Because, in Michael Lally's words, you will fill your heart with "so much gratitude that it overflows."

**VERSION TWO**

Do the same exercise described above, but this time make a list of what you're grateful for about your husband or life partner. This exercise is especially effective when you're mad at them.

It's a good idea to write at least one gratitude list in your journal every day. That way, when you're feeling low, you can go back and see how abundant your life really is. Or if you're at the end of your rope with your mate, you'll have written evidence of why the heck you're with them in the first place.

*chapter six*

# V Is for
# Voice Your *Desires*

---

## NOW WE'RE TALKING

*"At some point I realized that what I wanted
was a man I could have a conversation with—
in body, mind, and soul."*

—CLAIRE, TANGUERA

All right, I've found my inner goddess. I've learned how to listen. I've opened my heart. Do *I* ever get to talk? Do I get to have a voice in this dance? Or am I supposed to walk around with a blank happy smile on my face like a life-sized marionette while my guy pulls the strings.

The other night I danced with a new partner. He was a very nice man, but within about one minute after we had begun dancing, he tried to lead me into a high gancho (leg hook) in a way that would cause my thigh to wrap around his waist.

I didn't do it.

I could tell by his reaction that he just chalked up the fact I hadn't followed his lead to a misunderstanding. So he danced a few more steps, then tried once again to get me to do the gancho.

And again, I didn't do it.

So then he paused and said politely, in a helpful tone, "I'm trying to lead you to a gancho."

> "*Women must* dance. *They can't have a blank state of mind, like here I am, 'dance me.' The quality of the movement, the beauty of it, the sensuality, the musicality of it, actually the BIGGEST part of the dance, all these things, are* her *job . . . And the leader* wants *to hear your voice! Sharing the musical idea is like sharing a joke: If the follower doesn't react, it's like he's talking to a wall.*"
>
> —MILA VIGDOROVA, PROFESSIONAL TANGUERA

And I replied, very nicely, "I know."

He looked a bit bewildered and then asked (again, very politely), "Well, why aren't you doing it?"

And I replied (again, very nicely), "Because I've known you less than two minutes. I can assure you that I am NOT going to wrap my leg around your waist."

He looked kind of taken aback. And then he laughed, "Ha! I understand! Yes. I understand."

And from that point on, he kept his lead simple, fun, and appropriate to the setting and our level of friendship.

Now this happened just a few weeks ago, and I've been dancing and practicing the principles of L.O.V.E. for several years, so

I have tools. But if this had happened in my first few months of dancing, when I didn't know how to "voice my desires" in an effective way—i.e., a way that helps rather than hurts, a way that brings union rather than division—this interaction would have gone very differently. I might either have gone against my own desires—forcing myself to do the move my leader wanted me to while cringing inside, or I might have made him wrong by acting offended, or rolling my eyes, or even stopping the dance. But instead, I let him know what I wanted (and didn't want) in a friendly and respectful way, a way that came from a place of collaboration as opposed to competition, and I ended up getting what I wanted—a great dance.

## WHAT ARE YOU DANCING ABOUT?

Before I can effectively "voice my desire," I need to know what my desires *are*. What do I want? Do I want to exert control? Do I want power? Do I want to make war? Or do I want to make love?

The really great dancers don't kind of vaguely and tentatively pussyfoot around—they walk forward with *intention*. When they move, they're saying something. Even amateur dancers, if they're moving with intention, are compelling to watch. By the same token, even professional dancers can be boring if they lack this quality in their movement. It's the difference between merely going through the motions, or coming forward with a point of view.

*"It's really about the intention you're coming forward with. If it's that you want to convince the other person of your point of view, you've moved to power. And when you move out of love and into power, there's no winning—and there's no losing from a place of love."*

—DR. NICKI MONTI

A lot of acting technique is about intention. Intention is also often referred to as *objective*—as in, what is your character's *objective* in this scene?

Even a layman can usually tell the difference between good and bad acting. When it appears as if the actors are being *real* versus when it seems like they're just reciting memorized lines. If the actors seem like real people, rather than actors *acting* like real people, it's in large part because they know what the character's "intention" or "objective" is in the scene.

Roy London (my acting teacher) used to say that in any given script a character's objective will fall into two basic categories. They're seeking power or love.

For example, in the movie *Wall Street,* Michael Douglas's character Gordon Gekko is all about power. And in the movie *Casablanca,* Ingrid Bergman's Ilsa and Humphrey Bogart's Rick are all about love.

When I receive a script, the first thing I do is read and reread it until I understand the overall story of the piece. What is the script about? What are the character's objectives? Are they working to come together or split apart? Are they looking for connection? Or separation?

So, on the dance floor, before you give voice to your desires, the question to ask yourself is: What are you dancing for? What are you dancing about? What is your *intention* in this dance? Is your dance about power or love?

In the same way, when I'm communicating with my guy, I have to always remember what my intention is. Do I want to win a fight? Or do I want peace? Do I want to be right? Or do I want to be happy? Do I want to make love or war?

## KING OF THE ROAD

Have you ever heard of "road rage"? I am the poster girl. I'm the Danica Patrick of angry drivers.

I have *very* strong opinions about how other people should be driving (I know, you're *shocked* by that news), and I have no compunction about letting them know my opinions:

"Oh! Ahem! Sir! You cut me off!" HONK HONK! "Uh, HELLO? Have you ever heard of a TURN SIGNAL???? OK, LADY, the sign says the SPEED LIMIT'S fifty-five here, not 'MOSEY!'"

Luckily, my windows are usually rolled up while I'm shouting all this so the other drivers can't hear what I'm actually saying. They just see me muttering and gesturing angrily like a crazy person.

I also have the very bad habit of leaving just enough time to get where I'm going. Oh OK, I'll be honest, I'm usually running about ten minutes late.

Well, at one point, this behavior was not only making me a

stressed-out maniac, but I live in LOS ANGELES. People get SHOT for less! And one day I made another driver so mad with my honking that she punched my car. Oh, yes, while we were stopped at a stoplight she actually leaned out of her window and PUNCHED MY CAR WITH HER FIST! And this woman was HUGE. She was built like a truck driver—a truck driver whose hobby is BODYBUILDING. I'm lucky she didn't punch me in the head.

After that experience, I came to the conclusion that if I wanted to stay alive much longer I should probably change my ways. And, believe it or not, I looked to my husband as a role model. Even though in many ways he's just as feisty as I am, on the road he's a Zen master.

If someone is tailgating him, he pulls to the side, smiles, and gently waves to him or her to go ahead. If someone honks and yells at him (someone, um, who drives like *me,* for example), he simply waves and mouths, "Sorry!" as the driver speeds by. And since LA is known for its heavy traffic, he always leaves at least a half hour earlier than he needs to, so he's never in a stress-filled hurry to get to his destination.

Well, shortly after the bodybuilder/truck-driver-lady-punch-ing-my-car incident, I decided to give my guy's method a try. I had a meeting crosstown at ten A.M. This means rush hour. And in LA, from where I live, this means an hour and fifteen minutes travel time, if I'm lucky. My usual method would be to allow an hour and *five* minutes. Out of resentment. I mean, it's ridiculous, right? It simply should not take that long to drive across the city! But it does. So on this particular day I chose to actually *accept* reality. And "following my husband's lead," I left extra time. I left myself *two hours*! And the whole way there I waved the other drivers ahead of me if they wanted to pass or change lanes. I arrived happy, relaxed, and with a very nice feeling of superiority. "Those poor *late* people! If only they would just leave extra time for their commute like me. They wouldn't have to be so stressed out!" And not only did I get to my destination on time but early enough to hang out at the local Starbucks, read the morning paper, and drink a (decaf) soy latte.

> *"A rose is a rose is a rose."*
>
> —GERTRUDE STEIN

You may be asking yourself, "How does how you conduct yourself on the LA freeway relate to your relationship with your man? And what the heck does this have to do with partner dancing?" Well, everything actually. As Gertrude Stein said, "A rose is a rose is rose." If I'm aggressive on the road, you can be sure I'll be aggressive at the dry cleaner's, and if I'm aggressive at the dry cleaner's, you can be sure I will be aggressive at the grocery store, and if I'm aggressive there, you know I'll be aggressive on the dance floor. And yes, you see where I'm going here— if I'm aggressive on the dance floor you can bet your life I'm going to be aggressive at home.

Whatever my imbalances or shortcomings are as a person, they're going to show up everywhere in my life. If I want to have a loving and peaceful relationship with my man, I need to be nice to the barista at Starbucks. If I want to have a fun relationship with my dance partner, I have to be considerate to other drivers on the 405 Freeway. It's the trickle-up theory. My whole life is my practice floor. If I let the person with one item in their basket go ahead of me at the market, there's a better chance I'll be loving to my guy when I get home. Wherever I go, there I am. A fighter is a fighter is a fighter. A lover is a lover is a lover. A rose is a rose is a rose.

*"To learn to dance by practicing dancing or to learn to live by practicing living, the principles are the same."*

—MARTHA GRAHAM

One day I took a class in "leading" and I found out that leading is really hard! Not only is the leader doing the same dance moves as the follower, but he's *choreographing* the dance. He needs to find a way to be present with the follower in the current moment, but also has to be thinking a few moves ahead.

If, for example, his plan is to lead the follower into a *turn* after a few steps, he has to make sure there's room on the dance floor to safely execute the move. Yet he also has to be prepared to abort his plan at any time if the follower doesn't do the move he intended, or to avoid a collision if another couple suddenly appears in the dance pathway he has chosen. There's so much pressure!

When I led, I definitely suffered "performance anxiety." I was really concerned about my follower. I wanted her to have a good time. I didn't want to rush her or make her feel uncomfortable in any way. I wanted her to *like* me!

It was really fun when I was able to make my lead clear and see my follower respond to my lead with the move I intended. And when it looked like she was enjoying herself, I felt like a king! (Well, *queen*.)

But I also got a taste of how frustrating it is when a follower doesn't pay attention to my lead—if she gives me no feeling of *connection*. And I could tell that a few followers were *judging* the way I led—I could feel their disinterest in me and the moves I was leading. In other words, sometimes it felt like I was leading *myself*! It was like dance *karma*!

This experience really taught me how much responsibility the leader has on his shoulders. It gave me tremendous compassion for all leaders regardless of gender. But I think it's even harder for men. In addition to all the frustrations and difficulties I experienced as a leader, most guys I know really hate to look stupid in front of a woman. They want to appear, well, masculine. It takes a lot of courage to be willing to be a beginner—to allow yourself to flounder around and make mistakes—especially if it's in front of someone you want to impress.

My guy suffers from Boston Red Sox-itis. When it's World Series time, his symptoms are *severe*, and can be very hard to live with. I've been known to sit in my car listening to the sports news station to get the baseball scores so I can know what frame of mind he'll be in when I get home. If they lose, I know he'll be in a VERY BAD MOOD. It will be like coming home to a hibernating grizzly bear who has just been awakened too early from his winter nap. You want to keep your head down and your voice low.

But often, instead of leaving the grizzly bear alone, I would try to talk him out of his mood—to "make him feel better." I would say things like, "Honey, it's not that serious! It's just a game!"

And, of course, this would not only make my guy angrier, but

"*When I have a problem with my husband, or anyone really, I find that it works itself out rather quickly when I'm soft around it. Being soft around it means just to always remember that everyone is fighting their own battles. So the thing that's causing the conflict may not be our issue, as a couple, but one of those battles that they're fighting inside themselves—for sure those big reactions are their issues. And I find that if I just give them their space, that they're going to feel their issue, or hear it. If I resist—by arguing, for example—it doesn't give them a chance to hear it, to feel it, and process it."*

—SHANNON, TANGUERA

would often switch him from being mad about the game to being mad at me.

On the dance floor, I learned that if a leader had a problem executing a move he would often get very frustrated with himself. And in those moments I learned that the best thing I could do to help was to be patient and keep my mouth shut while he worked it out. When I did this, most of them were able to figure things out very quickly, and soon we'd be back to happily tripping the light fantastic.

In the same way, I realized that when my guy was stomping around the house in a rage because the Sox had lost to the Yankees in the ninth, the best thing I could do to "help him" was not try to talk him out of his feelings, but to let him work it out on his own.

I work through a lot of my problems in life by talking things over with my loving friends. But that's not my guy's way. Overly identifying with sports teams like the Boston Red Sox is just how he processes the frustrations in his life (and it seems a lot of guys do the same thing).

The Golden Rule is to "Do unto others as you would have them do unto you," but I think, at least in male/female relationships, it might be better to think of it as "Do unto others as they would have done unto *them.*"

I like therapy, and self-help books, and talking things over with friends. My guy likes to pop up a big batch of popcorn, and veg out in front of the TV watching ESPN. To each his own. And if I keep pestering him to "share" with me when he's in a bad mood, it's like poking a grizzly bear with a stick—chances are I'm going to get a big fat growl.

## ALWAYS WORK THE CONTEXT WITH THE CONTENT

I had a fascinating conversation with psychiatrist Dr. Philip Stutz about how couples can best communicate. He told me that good communication has two channels—*context* and *content.*

The *context* channel is always the same, which is: I love you, I respect you, I'm sensitive to you, I support you, I want you to feel good. The other channel is *content*. And content has to do with specifics. For instance, if your partner has a request, let's say they ask for your help with something, and you're busy, you can say: I can't help you now because I'm doing something else, or, I don't know how to help you, or, I can help you a little later—that part is the *content*. Dr. Stutz said that the important thing to remember is that "the *context* should always be an affirmation of the other person's value. That's really the secret of communication— because everyone wants to be validated, reassured, and loved. And if you don't do that in your communication with your partner *every time*, they feel deprived and angry—and you have the same reaction. If you don't work the context channel while in the content channel, the war is on."

> "*Nobody will ever win the battle of the sexes. There's too much fraternizing with the enemy.*"
>
> —HENRY KISSINGER

Like any couple, my guy and I have spats from time to time. And when we're in conflict, emotions get triggered. Once that happens, it's very difficult for me to work the *context channel*— or, another way to say it is, when I'm upset it's hard for me to stay in the *love*.

*Content* is tricky. While sometimes there are important issues we need to work out as a couple, very often, the thing we *think* we're fighting over isn't really what the fight's about at all.

When my guy and I first moved in together, I brought with me from my old apartment a little houseplant. It was about 99 percent dead, but for some reason I didn't want to throw it out. I felt strongly that with enough nurturing, it would spring back to life.

I kept the plant on the porch outside of my office, and one day I came home and it was gone. My guy had thrown it out.

You'd have thought from my reaction that he had thrown out my first-born child. I went INSANE!

Me: "Why did you throw out my *plant*?" Sob, sob, sob.

Him: "Um, it was dead?"

Me: "It wasn't dead! It was still *alive*!" Yell, sob.

Him: "It was dead! There was, like, one leaf! And it was BROWN!"

Me: "It's always about you! What *you* want! I live here too!"

Ah, so we were finally at the truth of it. My reaction wasn't about the plant. It was about me being afraid of losing my autonomy. The little plant was *me*.

When we first moved in together, my guy was in a much stronger financial position than I was and he was paying the lion's share of our bills. My intense reaction to the plant being thrown away had less to do with the plant, and more to do with my fear that not having financial independence in our relationship meant that I wouldn't have a voice. I was afraid that since I was making a lesser financial contribution, all my preferences and desires would be thrown away, just like that little plant.

But instead of letting my guy know what I was really afraid of—how vulnerable I felt about moving in together—I got caught up in the *content*. If I'd remembered the *context*—that my guy loved me and would never deliberately do something to hurt me, I might have gotten to the real truth of what I was upset about more quickly. I might have seen that just as sometimes a cigar is just a cigar, sometimes a dead plant is simply a dead plant.

Partner dance can be thought of as a model for *context*. It actively conveys messages of respect, love, and sexual attractiveness nonverbally, through physical actions—like eye contact, touch, etc. Whether it's a close embrace—where the dancers' bodies are actually pressed together, or an open one—where their arms are connected but there is space between them (the kind of embrace you see in most American ballroom-style dances like foxtrot), it's still an embrace. In this way, partner dancing provides an idealized example for male/female communication off the dance floor.

So when my guy and I are in conflict, it's essential that I stay connected to our *love*. Love is always the *context*; love is always the *intention*.

And I do this in the same way I stay connected on the dance floor. First of all I remember to breathe. The word "breathe" comes from the Latin "spiritus," so when I breathe in, I let the *spirit* of love in. And when I breathe out, I let fear leave me. I breathe in love. And I breathe out fear. And if I do this I can be sure that even if I have things to say that are uncomfortable or difficult to discuss—the spirit of love is with me. I can be honest about anything, as long as I do it with love.

# THE SECRET TO GETTING
# WHAT YOU WANT FROM A MAN
# (FOR WOMEN ONLY!)

To be completely honest, I *am* a little sexist. I feel that in many ways women are better than men. Throughout the centuries, we women have proven that we're equally adept at leading and following. While our men were off fighting battles, we women were home raising the kids, cooking the food, making the clothes, hunting the game, tending the fields, and even holding off the occasional band of marauding thieves and villains.

I think that in many ways women are better multitaskers than men, even our bodies are more flexible. And it may not be fair, or right—but maybe it's just because we're so darn CAPABLE— in relationships it seems most of the peace-making duties fall on the woman's shoulders. I mean, let's be honest, who is haunting the relationship self-help section of the local bookstore? Guys?

So, having said that, here's the top-secret *for-women-only* part of this book. Do not, I repeat DO NOT, show this part of this book to your husbands or boyfriends.

OK, I think we can all agree that (duh) criticizing your man doesn't work. So what the heck do we do? Well *I* think the best way to a man's heart is NOT through his stomach (and thank God, because if that was the case it would mean kissing the neighbor's cat at midnight for the rest of my New Year's Eves) but through his *ego*.

People LOVE to be praised! Don't you? I know that while I derive an intense amount of pleasure when I strap on my brand-

"*The easiest way to manipulate men is to praise them. Stroking their ego is the best way, because when you tell him how great it is when he does a certain thing, he will want to do it again.*"

—A TANGUERA

new purple patent leather tango shoes, it's even better when I arrive at the milonga and all the other tangueras go crazy for them too.

And the truth is the *good* guys really *do* want to be our knights in shining armor. But if we don't allow them to be, they feel like we don't need them. So the key is to make them THINK they're leading us, when in fact we are leading them! And how do we lead them? By praising them!

My guy always said things to me like: "You don't get it! When you criticize me and tell me what I'm doing wrong, I feel like a teenager being scolded by his mother and I want to rebel! If you'll just back off you'll probably get what you want."

And I would reply, "Well, you're not a teenager. Grow up! You should be able to hear me and not get so defensive!" And the fight would be on.

And I was right. It would have been absolutely fantastic if he'd been able to hear me and not get defensive. But you know what? He *couldn't*! So, I had a choice: I could walk around BY MYSELF knowing I was in the right, or I could BE PART OF A COUPLE and accept that he was who he was and was doing the best he

> "*When* you watch a couple dancing, the man is the one clearly in charge, but the woman is the one actually in charge."
>
> —JAIMES FRIEDGEN, PROFESSIONAL TANGUERO

could at the time, and instead of trying to change *him*, work on changing *myself*.

> "*You* can't always get what you want, but if you try sometimes, you just might find, you get what you need."
>
> —THE ROLLING STONES

On the dance floor, for at least the first minute or so, my intention is simply to connect with my partner, to "hear" what his rhythm is as a leader—to understand what he is saying.

Likewise, when I'm talking with my guy, especially if it looks like we're heading toward an argument, it's really important that I remember to listen carefully to what he is *really* saying, and not just his *words*. I need to hear what's *beneath* his words, which, when we're having a disagreement, most of the time is some version of, "I feel like you don't respect me."

Before I started working on the principles of L.O.V.E. in my relationship, when my temper showed signs of flaring up, I just let it rip! But now, when I feel my emotions getting hot, I pause, breathe in love, and remind myself of what my true objective is. What is my true desire in *any* interaction with my guy? If I can remember that even when we're disagreeing my objective is always to bring about union, closeness, and love, I stand a much better chance of using my voice in a way that helps rather than harms.

This doesn't mean I don't get to say my peace, or speak the truth, but whatever I say to my guy always has to have the quality of "I love you and I respect you." And I've found that if I start with that, most of the time, I may not necessarily get what I want, but I'll always get what I need.

"*The man is the head, but the woman is the neck; it turns the head.*"

—*MY BIG FAT GREEK WEDDING*

I have a friend who is also married to an actor, and she happens to make her living as a theater director. A marriage made in heaven, right? Wrong. Every time her husband had an audition, he and my friend would have a fight.

Before the audition, he would ask her to "run" the scene with him. Now "running a scene" can mean merely saying the lines with no real meaning, just to check if you have memorized them yet, or it could mean checking to see if your acting choices are effective.

So when my friend's husband asked her to "run" a scene with him, since she is a director, she assumed he wanted her feedback. She was after all an *expert*.

But instead of appreciating her feedback, every time her husband worked with her on a scene, it led to a fight. He'd always end up saying, "I don't want your advice! I know what I'm doing!"

My friend was so frustrated! She didn't know what her husband wanted from her. She was very respected in her career—her services as a director are in high demand—so why didn't her husband appreciate her advice?

One day we talked about it, and I realized that a solution might be found in the world of partner dancing. I suggested that perhaps her husband didn't want her services as a director. He didn't want that kind of feedback from her, what he wanted was more of what a good follower gives the guy she's dancing with. He wanted appreciation. He wanted her to make him feel like a good actor. What he really wanted from her was simply to hear, "That was great, honey!"

She protested, "But that's not honest! I'm a director! I need to be honest with him."

So I asked her, "Do you think he's a good actor?"

"Yes, of course. He's wonderful," she answered.

"So where's the dishonesty? Just try praising him. See what happens."

A couple of days later she called me up. "I followed your suggestion," she said.

"What happened?" I replied.

"Well, Jim and I ran the scene, and while we did it, I just took my director hat off. I didn't look at him critically in any way. I simply enjoyed his performance. And you know, he really *is* a good actor. So when we finished the scene, instead of suggesting different acting choices, different ways he could do it, I just said: 'Honey, that was great!'

"And he lit up. It was almost like he grew a bit physically. And wouldn't you know it? Then he asked me if I had any feedback!

So then we discussed the scene and thought of other ways he might try it. But it ended up that we both agreed his original way worked best. And it was so wonderful to feel like we'd collaborated. It was amazing to see that my old way of communicating was part of why we always had conflict. When I began by simply appreciating him, without just jumping in there with all kinds of unasked-for advice, it was like he felt respected, like I saw him as a fully capable man rather than a little boy who needed my help. What he really wanted was for me to believe in him. And by starting that way, with simply letting him know how much I respected him, I ended up actually getting what I wanted!"

So how do I voice my desires on the dance floor and at home with my guy? First I have to be aware of my desires—my intention. And my intention is always to come from love. And what are the qualities of love? One of the best and most beautiful descriptions I know is from the Bible:

*Love is patient; love is kind; love is not envious or boastful or arrogant or rude. It does not insist on its own way; it is not irritable or resentful; it does not rejoice in wrongdoing, but rejoices in the truth. It bears all things, believes all things, hopes all things, endures all things."*

—1 CORINTHIANS 13:4–7

If I always remember to come from love, I can be sure I'll always speak with my true voice.

*"Truth is like the sun. You can shut it out for a time,
but it ain't going away."*

—ELVIS PRESLEY

After I'd been dancing for several months, I started changing. I began to feel empowered in a very deep way. I became more confident. I even walked differently. I held myself straighter, moved more gracefully—people were starting to ask me, "Are you a dancer?"

But the change wasn't only physical. I was becoming stronger inside. I used to think that I needed certain conditions to feel safe and secure, be it a certain amount of money, or recognition in my career, or people's approval. As I became more and more adept at letting go of control, at opening my mind and body enough so that I could be led on the dance floor, I found that the truth I'd tried to bury deep down in my heart began to surface. I couldn't lie to myself any longer. I wanted to get married. Maybe for some people it was just a piece of paper, but not for me.

It was my guy's right to lead it the way he wanted to, but I was no longer happy with the dance of our relationship. And if I continued to live with him without being his wife, it was like continuing to dance with a leader whose style I was uncomfortable with—he had to assume that I liked it or why would I keep saying yes?

On the dance floor if I say no to a leader, he has a choice: He can move on to another partner or he can find out how he can alter his style so that it works for both of us, not just him. And if he won't, I shouldn't be dancing with him.

I realized that if I stayed in my relationship any longer without getting married I was being untrue to myself. I could no longer stay with my guy denying my own needs and desires because I was afraid that I wouldn't meet anyone else. Being alone and honest was better than trying to live a lie.

I needed to find my voice, my true one. I had tried to cajole, convince, nag, and complain, and it hadn't worked. But as the discoveries I was making on the dance floor changed me, my real and most powerful voice came up. And it came from my most real and powerful place, my femininity—my "inner goddess."

It turned out that my inner goddess was very gentle, but also very strong. She didn't need to convince or criticize to get her way. She was a woman of few words. Her actions spoke the loudest. She knew the only way for me to get out of a dance I didn't like was to leave the dance floor. If I wanted to be treated like a goddess, I needed to act like one. So I moved out. I traded our beautiful home in the mountains of Malibu for a furnished room in a girlfriend's apartment. And I didn't move out to punish my guy, or to try to manipulate him in any way, I did it because I could no longer let fear tamp down my true voice and my heart's desires.

It was the hardest thing I've ever done. But I knew I'd done the right thing, because I don't think you die of a broken heart, I think you die of a closed one. And as it turned out, rather than resulting in breaking up my relationship, being true to myself was the best thing I ever did to make it last.

## EXERCISES FOR
## VOICING YOUR DESIRES

### EXERCISE 1: WHAT DO YOU DESIRE?

As we discussed in this chapter, before you can voice your desires, you need to know what they are. So this exercise is about getting to know what you want. You'll use your journal in this exercise. Version One is for singles. Version Two is for singles or for those already in a relationship.

### VERSION ONE

*"The Man I Love"*

(It's preferable to do this exercise when you're not dating anyone.)

Take out your journal and write five qualities that your dream man would possess. When you make this list, have fun! The qualities that pop into your head might seem silly, or not even make sense to you. Don't worry. Just write down whatever comes to mind. You'll do this every day for two weeks. Each time you make a new entry, make sure you

*continues*

don't look back at what you wrote the day before. Each day, start fresh with whatever pops into your head. And don't worry if there are repeats.

A first list might look like this:

Dark hair  •  Great sense of humor  •  Is a great cook  •  Loves to buy me presents  •  Loves to read

And the next list might look like this:

Loves to buy me presents  •  Wants to get married  •  Smart  •  Loves to dance  •  Blond hair

And the next might look like this:

Dark hair  •  Wants to get married  •  Loves to buy me presents  •  Smart  •  Great sense of humor

Do the list for two weeks. At the end of the two weeks, go through all your lists and pick the top five qualities. If they are important to you, they will probably have repeated over the two weeks, as did "wants to get married" in the lists above. This is your "What I Want in a Man" template. What's great about making this list is that you know what your real "type" is. The one that is your true heart's desire, rather than one that only relies on sexual chemistry.

I made this list when I was single (yes, it's the one I referred to in the yurt story). And it turned out that my guy matched my final list perfectly, except for the "wants to get married" part. And that turned out to be a non-negotiable area for me. The other quality he fell a bit short on was the "loves to buy me presents." Don't get me wrong, he really does love to buy me presents, it's just that he likes to buy them at the 99-cent store. And while I really do subscribe to the "it's the thought that counts" philosophy, and find it adorable when my guy surprises me with *any* gift, there's just so many feather dusters, lint rollers, and miniature flashlights a girl needs.

Note to self: Next time I make a wish list be *specific*. For example:

"Loves to buy me presents at Tiffany's."

**VERSION TWO**

If you're already in a relationship, you can do the same exercise described above on any aspect of your life. For example, if you feel a lack of purpose, you can make lists of things you think you might enjoy doing.

Your first list might look like this:

- Volunteer at a hospice • Start a vegetable garden
- Start a weekly poker game with friends
- Learn CPR • Learn the Argentine tango

As with Version One, do this exercise every night for two weeks and then pick your top five and do one of the things on your list. If it doesn't end up making your heart sing, try the next item on your list.

# chapter seven

# E Is for Embrace Your *Partner*

---

## HOLD ME TIGHT AND
## NEVER LET ME GO

Learning to follow another person's lead on the dance floor changed my life. I began to listen more deeply in all areas of my life. My heart opened so much that I couldn't ignore its inner longings. And once they were out in the open, my desires demanded a voice.

As a result I was able to hear and accept that my guy wasn't ready to get married, but I knew in my heart that I *was*.

I gave voice to my truth gently, meaning I really didn't need to say much; my action of moving out and moving on spoke much louder than any words.

Now, here is how the story was supposed to go:
The night I move out, my guy can't sleep, because something is missing: ME! He tosses and turns, as the bedsheets tangle and wrap around him like ropes. Through his long dark night of the soul he's visited by the ghosts of his romances past, present, and future. Oh, wait . . . that's Dickens's *A Christmas Carol*!

He thinks about his future prospects. They are *chilling*. He's an old man, dying, alone in his bed. His gnarled hand opens and a round object rolls out onto the floor. It's a snow globe! He moans. Then, in barely a whisper says the word, "Rosebud . . ." Oh wait, that's *Citizen Kane* . . .

OK, how about this: He can't stand being without me for one moment longer! He throws on his clothes and drives like a madman out in the dark night to where I'm staying. HE MUST HAVE ME BACK! He pounds on my friend's apartment door DEMANDING to see me! I open the door—tears streaming down my cheeks—he looks at me and melts, he's so grateful to see me tears are spilling down his cheeks too—and he says, "I'm sorry."

"Don't," I reply. "Love means never having to say you're sorry."

Oh, wait, that's *Love Story*.

O K. Here's how the story actually went. When I moved out, I knew I'd done the right thing, but I was also still deeply in love with my guy. And while I moved out because I felt that I had no other choice—it was the only way to be true to myself— I was still hoping that he'd miss me so much he'd break down and ask me to marry him. But he didn't.

The days went by, and turned into weeks, then. . . . OK, OK! I'm lying! After my good-for-me-I-finally-did-the-right-thing feeling of bravado wore off, you guessed it, my *dreaded neediness* kicked in! So, the *very* night of the day I moved out, I called him:

Him: "Hello?"

Me: "Why aren't you calling me?"

Him: "What?"

Me (crying): "WHY AREN'T YOU CALLING ME?"

Him: "Um, because you broke up with me?"

Me (sobbing loudly): "BUT YOU'RE SUPPOSED TO MISS ME!"

Him: "But I DO miss you, honey, only you said that we were broken up? I don't understand . . ."

Me: "BUT YOU'RE SUPPOSED TO MISS ME SO MUCH THAT YOU BEG ME TO COME BACK!" (SOB, choked breathing, SOB)

Him: "Well, of course I want you back! Come home!"

Me (sniff, calmer): "But, are we *engaged?*"

Him (long pause): "Honey, I told you . . . I'm sorry. But I'm just not ready yet."

Me (SOB): "THEN STOP CALLING ME!" (Sob.) "JUST LEAVE ME ALONE!"

Him (gently): "Um . . . *you* called me."

Me: "Oh."—SOBBING—"but I *miss* you!"


Yeah I know, so much for my "inner goddess." Apparently she was out having a drink with Aphrodite and Athena at the time.

And I would love to tell you that in just a couple of weeks we were back together—that my guy quickly realized the error of his ways and sent me a dozen roses with a big fat engagement ring attached with a ribbon. But it didn't happen that way. Nope. It took him TWO MONTHS to come to his senses! And rather than running around enjoying my newfound single freedom, I cried myself to sleep almost every night.

*"Life isn't about waiting for the storm to be over, it's about learning how to dance in the rain."*

—UNKNOWN AUTHOR

While I was separated from my guy, I kept up my tango dancing. It kept me grounded in my conviction to be true to my desires and to *myself.* And while at first I stood up for what I wanted in my old sobbing, snorting, needy, uncool way, at least I did it. And my willingness to take that action allowed my "inner" goddess to begin to manifest herself in my outward life as well.

During that time I met a tanguero who really taught me the importance of showing up for your heart's desire, no matter what.

He was a well-known tango teacher in LA named Mark Celaya. His usual partner was busy with work, so he asked me if I was interested in being his practice partner. Honored that he would think I was good enough, I quickly said, "Yes!"

Our partnership was strictly platonic—he was in a happy long-term relationship and he knew that even though we had broken up, I was still in love with my guy. We agreed to meet every Tuesday at a local gym to practice our tango technique.

By about the second week, Mark shared something with me. He was a cancer survivor. He explained that the chemo and radiation he'd received had been very hard on his body, and as result he had nerve damage in his feet. But ever the optimist, Mark told me that he was actually glad about it, that since his feet were numb he "never had to suffer from foot pain after too many hours of practice!"

Then around week three of our practice sessions, he revealed something else. During our practices, Mark always wore inside his shirt collar a small towel wrapped around his neck. Since Mark, like most tangueros, was very fastidious about the way he dressed, I'd always assumed the towel was there to absorb perspiration while we worked. But on this particular day, he pulled the towel aside and showed me the real reason he always wore it. There was a large, bruised-looking tumor on the side of his neck. The tumor was about the size of a tangerine. By week seven, it had grown to the size of a grapefruit. His cancer had come back.

After our eighth, and what turned out to be our final, week of practice, I hugged Mark good-bye and walked outside to go to my car. I didn't know it then, but it was the last time I'd ever see him.

Mark was the kind of guy who showed up for his life—including his passion for dancing the tango—no matter what. He taught me that we only have a finite time here on earth, so if you love to dance, do it. And do it full-out. For as long as you can.

That same day, as I walked across the parking lot to my car, I was surprised to see my guy's car pull up next to me. I went up to his window and saw that he was dressed in a suit and tie—which was strange as he usually dresses in jeans and T-shirts.

So I asked, "What are you doing here? How come you're all dressed up? Do you have an audition?"

He didn't answer but just got out of his car, and then I saw that he was holding two dozen long-stemmed red roses. And right there in the parking lot, he got down on one knee on the asphalt,

*My husband, Kip Gilman, proposing to me in the parking lot of Bally's gym, North Hollywood.*

> "[The saying is] 'It takes two to tango.' Why not two to cha-cha, or two to swing? Why two to tango? Because two makes one."
>
> —CARLOS GAVITO, TANGUERO

held out the flowers and a little black box that contained a beautiful vintage diamond and ruby ring, and asked me to marry him.

I practically screamed, "YES!"

Some strangers in the parking lot, who had seen the whole thing play out, honked their horns in approval. And my guy and I came together in the happiest embrace I've ever experienced.

Our wedding was very different from my first one. Since my guy and I had had big fancy expensive weddings the first time around, we wanted to make sure that ours was simple, full of love, and most important, FUN!

Rather than the Hotel Bel-Air, we chose for our nuptials a rent-by-the-hour chapel in Las Vegas. For romantic atmosphere, instead of swans and harps, we had a plastic arch decorated with plastic flowers. Instead of celebrity guests, there were framed pictures of Liberace and Elvis Presley on the walls. And instead of a supreme court judge, we were married by a justice of the peace dressed in a cobalt blue double-breasted suit, who looked like a lost member of Gladys Knight's Pips. In other words, it was *perfect*.

In attendance were my parents, a favorite aunt and uncle, my beautiful soon-to-be stepdaughter, and two of my closest friends.

My dad sang, my husband played guitar, and I wept. And after the ceremony, when the pastor pronounced us "husband and wife," we blasted Elvis's "Viva Las Vegas" on a boom box that we'd brought with us for the occasion. And to my frugal husband's delight, it only cost $49.95 for the whole shebang (plus a tip for the pastor).

After the ceremony, everyone laughed and cried and talked about how it was the best wedding they'd ever been to. The pastor had to finally kick us all out because he had "another wedding scheduled in fifteen minutes."

Then, instead of retiring to an elegant candlelit dinner at a fancy restaurant, the whole wedding party went to an all-you-can-eat buffet. It was fantastic. Me, fresh from the chapel in my floor-length ivory satin strapless gown, standing in line waiting to pile my cheap ceramic just-out-of-the-steam-cleaner plate high with crab legs and jumbo shrimp.

But whatever our choice of after-ceremony restaurants lacked in ambience, it made up for in heart. And whenever our guests clanked their stainless steel cutlery against their water glasses, we kissed with the innocence and happiness of the newlyweds we were.

It was an absolutely happy, kooky, wonderful wedding. The one I would have dreamed of my whole life if I'd only had enough imagination. And yes, in contrast to my first wedding, a real "marriage" took place that day.

"*In* tango there are moments when you lose track of who's leading and who's following. You're dancing and you think, 'Oh I just wanted to do something to this part of the music and he just led it,' and then you think, 'Did I lead it or did he lead it?' And it's not even important, because in this moment it's like you're submerged in the music—you're hearing it the same way—you're doing it together. And I think in a good relationship it's kind of the same thing."

—MILA VIGDOROVA, PROFESSIONAL TANGUERA

The goal of partner dancing is to reach such a feeling of connection that there's no longer a leader or a follower—but that two really dance as one. Sometimes when you're dancing, you feel so connected to your partner it's like everything else in the room and even in your outside life slips away. Maybe you had a successful day at work or maybe you had a fight with your boyfriend but suddenly the temperature of the room, and maybe even your partner's cologne, or what shoes you're wearing, or if you believe in astrology maybe it's how the planets in the heavens are aligned that day—all these things coalesce into this magic moment that allows you to have this deep soul connection with another human being.

It's like that scene from the movie *West Side Story*, when Tony and Maria see each other for the first time at the dance and everything falls away—the music and the other dancers—and suddenly it's just the two of them touching each other's palms on a dance floor.

In those rare times when you're lucky enough to have this feeling with your partner, it's like no one is leading and no one is following, but more like the music is indeed playing *you*. And while you're embracing each other, it's like you're also being embraced by the music, and all the other dancers on the floor, and in some way by the entire world.

And I think this—more than the sensual movements, the beautiful music, the fun and the camaraderie, and even (gasp!) the shoes!—is the thing that keeps us dancers coming back again and again to the dance floor. This feeling of connection with another human being. This is the part, I believe, that's the real model for relationships off the dance floor. It's this shared connection— where it's almost like you can read each other's minds, or even that you're really *one* mind—this feeling of being connected to something else, something bigger, something eternal. It's the feeling some people say they get from meditation or prayer. And yes, I think this moment is an expression of a kind of love, but it's the transcendent kind, the kind that never dies.

I think that, like my friend Mark, we who love to dance commit to the dance itself, no matter what. Even if we go out dancing and on that particular night we don't get to feel this kind of blissful connection—we show up anyway. We still come back to the dance floor again and again, so that we're available for the possibility. And again, I believe this is a metaphor for relationship.

> "*It's* this perfect timing of these two hearts that open to each other at that very moment at that place and time . . . it's like this perfect moment where you lose yourself in the other, but you don't lose yourself in yourself . . . but there's this illusion that you can hold on to this moment forever, but you have to let it go. And this is to me the metaphor of life, right? I think that the lesson in this incredible connection that you have sometimes is a gift, and you know, life is a gift, but you have to let go. I know it's very sad, it's very tragic, because there is a part of us that wants to be eternal."
>
> —LUIZA PAES, PROFESSIONAL TANGUERA

When you marry, or make any deep commitment to another person, you're not so much making a commitment to the person as an individual but to the relationship itself—to the dance that is created by your union.

I continue to look to my parents' marriage as a model for the kind of long-term commitment I'm talking about. I grew up watching my parents dance together. Since they're both professionals, they really know what they're doing on the dance floor.

*Tango bliss at Milonga El Floridita, Los Angeles.*

But it isn't their fancy moves that make them look so beautiful when they dance together, it's their *connection* with each other that has always taken my breath away.

My dad has suffered some health problems in the last few years. Recently he was in the hospital for a serious procedure and I stayed with my mom in his hospital room while he rested in recovery. As we waited for him to wake up, my mom told me a little story.

"Something happened the other night I think you'll get a kick out of. I was in the kitchen cooking dinner, and your dad was in his recliner watching a KCET special about the Big Band era. While I was cooking, I started dancing around a little to the music, and I glanced over at your dad and saw that he was in his chair tapping his feet to the music too.

"I kept cooking and dancing by myself, and then I saw your dad get up from his chair and start moving to the music in front of the TV. As I watched him, he turned and caught my eye. And as we looked at each other, still dancing individually to the music, we smiled and came together until we were in each other's arms dancing in the living room. It was such a nice moment."

My mom teared up a little. And so did I. She looked over at my dad as he slept in his hospital bed. She looked worried.

I said, "It's OK, Mom, you don't have to keep staring at him. He's resting. He's OK."

She kept her eyes riveted on him and said, "I know him so well that I can tell just by looking at him how he's feeling."

Just then, my dad stirred and his mouth grimaced slightly. Mom leapt up immediately, and adjusted his pillow.

My dad opened his eyes and smiled up at her and murmured, "Thanks, honey. That's better."

Mom smiled back at him and kissed him on the forehead. Then sat back down, smiled at me, and said, "See?"

Now that I've been with my husband for over ten years (five and a half as his wife, but who's counting?), I'm getting a taste of what a long-term relationship is. My parents have been married over fifty years, they've been together virtually their entire adult lives, and they have a friendship and bond that most people can only dream of.

I'm beginning to feel that kind of bond with my husband. He's truly my best friend. And as I said in the Introduction, there is no one I would rather be stranded with on a desert island. All I would need is him. And some SPF 70 sunblock. And a wide-brimmed hat. And, OK, my iPod. And my dance shoes. And maybe I could make a little dance floor out of bamboo or something.

As I said earlier, sometimes the best dancers are the ones who are skilled enough to move with such subtlety that the only ones aware of the intricacy of their dancing are the dancers themselves. But they are so *connected* with each other, you can't take your eyes off them. And as the years have gone by, the dance I share with my husband has gotten more subtle too—it's become quieter, just for us. I've watched my parents dance together for fifty years and counting, and I want to be just like them, gliding and twirling through life with my husband for as long as we can.

"*Dancers are the athletes of God.*"

—ALBERT EINSTEIN

"*Dancing comes down to love—how to recognize it, how to give it, and how to accept it . . . the love you come to know is the big-picture kind, the Mother Teresa kind, the stuff of what makes us human, the true reason it will be a tragedy if we blow ourselves up with nukes or die off from global warming.*"

—SAMANTHA DUNN, WRITER, SALSA DANCER

LEFT: *Kip and me, Christmas 2009.* ABOVE: *Mom and Dad today.*

# CONNECTION EXERCISES

### EXERCISE 1: MIRRORING

This is an exercise that I sometimes give my acting students. For this exercise you will need three people. The ones doing the "mirroring" are called partners A and B, and the third person is the "caller."

The partners face each other standing about two feet apart. The caller sits (or stands) nearby in a place where she can see both partners.

The caller allows the partners to just look at each other for a few moments before starting, then, when the partners appear ready, the caller chooses who will lead first by calling out either A or B.

If she is chosen as the leader, B will start slowly moving a part of her body and A will attempt to follow B's movements as if she is her mirror image.

B must make sure to move slowly enough so that A can stay with her.

If B moves so quickly that A can't follow her movements, it spoils the game.

The caller lets B lead for a while and then calls out "A," and the partners switch the lead.

The caller lets the game go on for a while and then says, "Switch." And the partners continue to mirror each other.

As the game goes on, the caller starts to call out, "Switch," more and more quickly, until finally the caller says, "On your own."

At that point the partners begin to change the lead on their own, without being prompted by the caller.

When this is done with full concentration, at this point the caller should not be able to tell who's leading and who's following.

Now give the caller a chance to be a mirror partner.

This exercise provides a great example of what it feels like to be truly connected with your partner in a lead/follow dance. Do this exercise as often and for as long as you like.

*continues*

### EXERCISE 2: SHUT UP AND DANCE!

Now it's time to put on some music and dance! Dance like one of your goddesses! Dance like Ellen DeGeneres! Dance like Michelle Obama! Dance like the terpsichorean goddess you are!

Or perhaps by now I've inspired you to go out and try a little partner dancing of your own. To help you on your journey, at the back of this book I've included a short primer describing some of the more popular social partner dances like salsa, tango, and swing, as well as a list of resources—teachers, dance studios, shoe suppliers, and so on, to help you get out there and get your partner dance groove on! I look forward to seeing you on the dance floor!

# *Epilogue*

Have you noticed it yet? There's something missing in this book. Where is the story of my going dancing with my husband? Ah. Well. Here's the thing: My guy happens to be a great dancer, *but* he likes to dance "freestyle"— he prefers to dance to the beat of his own drummer. When I first started dancing, he came with me to a few tango classes, and he hated it. He just didn't have the patience. So remembering my mom's famous "Pick your battles!" I decided to let it go.

But then while writing this book, it came up again. And I realized the book just wouldn't be complete unless I talked about dancing with my husband! So, I thought to myself, "I need to pick a dance where we're both beginners so we will be on the same level, so tango is out." Then I remembered I always wanted to learn West Coast swing! Perfect!

So I broached the subject:

"Honey, you want my book to be good, right?" (I know, I know, I slid into the subject manipulatively—what's he going to say when I put it like that? No?)

He looked at me skeptically. (He knows me very well.)

"Um, yes . . ." he added, clearly thinking, "Where is she going with this?"

"Well, I realized in order to write this book I need us to dance together. There's a West Coast swing class tonight, right near *us*!"

"No," he said, "there's a game on tonight. I've been looking forward to it all day."

"Well, can't you record it, honey? I mean, how do I explain why I don't go dancing with my husband? It's a *glaring* omission. It's for my *book*!"

Pause. Pause. Pause. We look at each other. My parents both were in sales when they weren't performing. I know that when you're trying to close a deal, the first one who speaks, loses!

Pause, pause, pause. (I ain't saying a word.)

"Oh . . . OK."

"Honey!" I throw my arms around his neck and kiss him. "It's going to be so much fun!"

"Yeah," he grumbles, as he sets the DVR, "I'm sure."

We arrive at the Cowboy Grill. It's a cavernous place with pool tables, big flat-screen TVs, and a huge dance floor. Seventies music blares from speakers set all around the room. Instead of the ubiquitous disco ball, a mirror-encrusted saddle hangs high above the dance floor.

My husband and I grab a table.

A group of dancers whirl to "Color My World," occasionally flinging their arms out gracefully as they move. They're doing a dance called "Nite Club" that encourages a lot of dramatic *Saturday Night Fever*–inspired arm movements.

My guy surveys the dancers. There's a lot of moussed hair, tight white stretch jeans, and rhinestones out there. He looks worried.

OK, women line up on the kitchen side, men on the bar side. It's time for the beginning West Coast swing lesson." The dance teacher is around sixty and is wearing a kerchief around his neck, holding a microphone up to his mouth.

I look to my guy. He smiles and gamely takes his place for the lesson. He is the tallest and most handsome man on the dance floor. I can almost feel the single women licking their chops. I feel proud. "He's mine," I think to myself, gloating.

"OK, ladies, here's your basic pattern: right step, left step, left right left, then step back on a left right left. Step step, triple-step triple-step—step step triple-step triple-step. OK, practice that while I teach the men."

I see my guy across the dance floor, shuffling his feet, trying hard to emulate the teacher. As I watch him, I feel like I'm falling in love with him all over again.

"M'aam, *m'aam*! Please pay attention," the dance instructor calls to me. Everyone is looking at me. I realize while all the other women are practicing the dance, I'm standing there like a lovesick teenager staring at my husband.

"Sorry!" I call out, taking my place back in the line of women. My husband laughs.

"OK, find a partner," the teacher calls out.

My guy and I walk toward each other giggling and come together in a dance embrace. We dutifully practice the steps as the teacher commands. We're cracking up. We're having a great time.

The class is structured in such a way that the partners rotate every couple of minutes. I enjoy glancing over and seeing my husband gamely practicing his moves. He looks about twelve years old as he gazes up at the teacher to make sure he's getting it right, gingerly leading his partners, earnestly attempting to execute the patterns correctly.

After a while, we finally end up together again in the rotation.

"I'm not sure if I'm getting this," he says apologetically. But then he leads me beautifully through the steps we've just learned.

I feel a little swoony. He really is a wonderful dancer.

After the lesson we take a seat at the bar, nursing a couple of Diet Cokes while we watch the other couples practicing. There is a TV mounted over the bar, and the football game is on.

"Oh my God! They came back and won it! I can't believe I missed it!" he says, not angrily at all, but clearly disappointed.

I look at the dance floor and notice a couple dancing really beautifully together.

"Look, honey, look! Those dancers are fantastic!"

"I will, honey, I will. Just give me a minute, they're doing a replay."

He watches the TV, transfixed by the replay of the game.

I look back at the dancers and am once again struck by the beauty of their movements. I start to say something again, but then I look at my husband and see how much joy he seems to be having watching the game.

And in that moment I realize that it isn't necessary to force my guy to take dance lessons with me. I don't have to force him to participate in a passion he doesn't share, just as he would never force me to sit in front of the TV with him during the World Series or football season (or the Super Bowl, or the U.S. Open, or the Masters, or just about any sport on earth, even curling, well, maybe not curling, even my sports fanatic husband has limits).

And maybe this is a big part of why our relationship works so well, because we're able to accept each other for who we are as individuals. We allow each other to enjoy our separate passions. I think about this while we sit together—holding hands and drinking our Cokes—his eyes on the football game, mine on the dancers, as they twirl and spin beneath that crazy mirrored saddle.

# Resources

## Shut Up and Learn to Dance!

In this book I've concentrated on the Argentine tango, but there are so many other wonderful partner dances to explore. In addition to the tango, I also love to dance salsa, West Coast swing, and lindy.

When considering which partner dance you want to try, the first thing to think about is the music. Do you love rock and roll? Rhythm and blues? Funk? Does the Brian Setzer Orchestra or Benny Goodman send you over the moon? Or maybe you love the Buena Vista Social Club? Marc Anthony? Or are you a rabble-rousing country girl at heart? No matter what your favorite music style is, there is a complementary partner-dance style to fit it—yes, even rap and Lady Gaga!

## A VERY SHORT PRIMER ON SOME POPULAR PARTNER DANCE STYLES

(Special thanks to San Manh for permission to borrow heavily from his excellent website justdanceballroom.com when compiling this list.)

### SWING

Swing dancing is usually characterized by its bounce and energy as well as by lots of spins or underarm turns. There are hundreds of variations, but when most people refer to basic swing dancing, they are referring to a simplified version of the original lindy hop, favoring six-count moves and also referred to as six-count swing, East Coast swing, jitterbug, and lindy.

Six-count swing can be danced to jazz or Big Band music. The six-count basic can be modified in many ways, but it is most common as rock-step; triple-step, triple-step (often referred to as triple-time or triple-step swing); or rock-step, step, step (often referred to as single-step or single-time swing). Six-count swing is easy to learn, especially when done with the single-step rhythm. The triple-step rhythm is better suited for slower songs, and can be substituted for the single-step once you are comfortable with the steps.

### WEST COAST SWING

West Coast swing is a smooth and sexy dance style that is danced in a slot (or narrow line), making it perfect for a crowded dance floor. It consists of six-beat and eight-beat patterns and can be danced to different kinds of music, including rock, blues, funk, country-and-western, disco, and contemporary pop. West Coast swing also stresses the leader-follower connection and dancing in close harmony with the music. (Note: Next to Argentine tango, it's my favorite partner dance.)

### SALSA

Salsa is a distillation of many Latin and Afro-Caribbean dances. Each of the latter played a large part in salsa's evolution. It's similar to mambo in that both have a pattern of six steps danced over eight counts of music. The dances share many of the same moves. In salsa, turns have become an important feature, so the overall look and feel are quite different from that of mambo. Mambo generally moves forward and backward, whereas salsa has more of a side-to-side feel.

### AMERICAN BALLROOM

This category includes the dances you see on the television show *Dancing with the Stars* or in the movie *Take the Lead.* It includes dances such as the Viennese waltz, paso doble, quick step, and so on. If dancing like Ginger Rogers in an old black-and-white musical is your fantasy, then definitely try ballroom.

For a more comprehensive description of partner dance styles, check out justdanceballroom.com or arthurmurray.com, or do a Google search for the specific dance style you're interested in.

## RESOURCES (DANCE FESTIVALS, INSTRUCTORS, AND MORE)

There are opportunities to learn to dance all over the United States as well as internationally. In addition to dance studios and clubs, dance festivals and congresses are great places for you to learn. There you'll have a chance to meet other dancers and have the opportunity to study with some of the best dancers and teachers from all over the world. Also, many of the top dance instructors in the United States are constantly doing guest workshops in other cites. So no matter if an instructor is based in New York or Los Angeles or even Buenos Aires, there's a good chance that he may be teaching at some point in a community near you.

Below is a partial list of websites to get you started. Remember, even if dance studios or instructors are located in a different state, check them out anyway because they may be traveling soon to a city near you or can direct you to professionals in your area. You could also try doing an Internet search of the dance you are interested in, adding your city and/or state. Just start exploring. My experience has been that if you just start to *seek,* you'll usually find what you're looking for—or maybe something even better!

### TANGO

All the professional dancers and teachers mentioned and quoted in this book and listed in the acknowledgments section can be found through the Internet. Most have websites or are on Facebook. Also be sure to search their names on YouTube for performance videos.

In the meantime, here are some tango websites to start you off!

## GENERAL INFO ABOUT CLASSES, MILONGAS, AND MORE

**newyorktango.com:** Richard Lipkin's tango page, this site has lots of information about tango in New York City and other areas.

**tangoafficionado.com:** This wonderful site was founded by Vladimir Estrin (who is quoted in this book). Here you can find out everything that's happening in tango in the Los Angeles area and across the country.

**tangobeat.com:** Another great site for information about tango in the United States and around the world.

**tangoinfoba.com.ar:** A good site for general information about the Argentine tango and travel to Buenos Aires.

**tejastango.com:** This is a great site that has links to tango resources across the United States and internationally.

**todotango.com**: A fantastic website. It contains all kinds of fascinating information about the Argentine tango—the history, the music, the famous personalities like Carlos Gardel. Definitely check it out.

And here is contact info for the tango goddesses quoted extensively in this book who also teach:

**Julie Friedgen**: tangolosangeles.com and Facebook
**Luiza Paes:** Facebook
**Silvina Valz:** Facebook
**Mila Vigdorova:** milatango.com and Facebook

## TANGO IN BUENOS AIRES

If you have the time and money, I can't think of a better way to learn to dance tango than through a trip to Buenos Aires. Here are some people I can personally vouch for who provide tango tours to Buenos Aires.

**Becca Tango Tours:** Becca Fabian (quoted in this book) and her husband, Caro Minas, own a beautiful apartment building in Buenos Aires. They rent out rooms and conduct personalized tango tours. Visit their beautiful website for more information: beckatangotours.com.

**Connection Sur Tango Clinic:** Makela Brizuela is a dear friend, a fantastic tango teacher, and a *porteña* (a female native of Buenos Aires). In addition to her classes in the Los Angeles area, she offers a tango tour to Buenos Aires once a year. Go to her website makelatango.com for more information.

**Tango Experience**: Also *porteños*, Oliver Kolker and his partner Silvina Valz (quoted in this book) are two of my favorite tango teachers in the world. Oliver has been offering tango tours to Buenos Aires since 2005. Go to tangoexperience.com for more information.

## MISCELLANEOUS BUENOS AIRES INFO

**Caserón Porteño:** In Buenos Aires there are "tango houses," which are like bed-and-breakfasts only they cater to tango tourists. They usually offer a daily tango lesson as part of their amenities.

When I went to Buenos Aires, I stayed at a great one, the Caserón Porteño. The lodgings were wonderful and very reasonably priced, and the innkeepers made me feel like family. I highly recommend staying there if you plan to travel to Buenos Aires on your own. Their website is caseronporteno.com.

**Mansion Dandi Royal:** Another wonderful place to stay in Buenos Aires that comes highly recommended is the Mansion Dandi Royal.

I haven't stayed there yet myself, but I hope to soon. Even if you don't stay there, it's worth checking out their beautiful website: mansiondandiroyal.com.

Here are the sites of some great teachers and places to study in Buenos Aires (remember, most of these teachers are constantly traveling to the United States and other countries, so check their sites to see if they will be coming to your area).

**Claudia Codega and Esteban Moreno**: Another amazing Buenos Aires–based tango couple who I've had the pleasure of studying with here in the United States. Their website is estebanyclaudia .com.

**DNI Tango**: My favorite tango school in Buenos Aires. If you go, give owner Dana Frígoli a big kiss from me! The website is dni-tango .com.

**Melina Brufman and Claudio Gonzalez**: Look this couple up on YouTube. They will blow your mind! And not only are they gifted dancers, they are also incredible teachers. I have studied with them at many festivals here in the United States. I adore them, and I know you will too. Their website is tangopulenta.com.

## TANGO FESTIVALS

Go to tangobeat.com for a comprehensive list of tango festivals in the United States and worldwide, but here are some great tango festivals I have attended personally or which other people have recommended.

Chicago tango week: Chicagotangoweek.org
Portland Tango Fest: Claysdancestudio.com
The Smith: Santamonicatangofestival.com
Tango Mundo: Tangomundofestival.com

## TANGO SHOES

OK, I'll admit it. A huge part of my love of the Argentine tango has to do with the shoes. Here are some of my favorite tango shoe pushers, um, I mean, *suppliers*:

**Axis Tango**: I bought my purple patent-leather shoes with orange patent leather straps from Gaia and Chris of Axis Tango. Need I say more? They offer Comme Il Faut, Neo Tango, and Greta Flora. Contact them at info@axistango.com or on Facebook.

**Maleva Shoes**: I'm on my fourth pair of Comme Il Fauts from Jennifer Bratt's great site. Great selection, great customer service, and occasional sales! Go to malevashoes.com.

**Tango Splash**: Yolanda Rossi is a beautiful and elegant Grande Dame of the LA tango scene and has exquisite taste. In addition to tango classes and events, she offers a great selection of gorgeous tango shoes and clothes. Contact her at tangosplash.com.

Some other great tango shoe sites are julia-bella.com, felinashoes.com, and diva-boutique.com.

## SWING

Doug Silton is one of the best swing dancers I know—he's expert in all styles: West Coast, lindy, balboa—and he's an excellent teacher. I've had several private lessons with him myself so I can recommend him highly. He also has a lot of great videos and other resources available on his website, dougsilton.com.

Trish Connery is one of the best West Coast swing teachers out there. She also teaches hustle, salsa, and many other dances. Her website is dancechatter.com.

A great resource for information about swing dancing is the World Swing Dance Council. Their website is www.swingdancecouncil.com. There they have listings of instructors and events across the country.

## SALSA

Laura Canellias is one of the most accomplished salsa dancers and teachers I've ever met. Definitely check out her site and study with her if you can: salsadivaprod.com.

Albert Torres has been a salsa promoter for years. He hosts salsa dance congresses all over the United States and internationally. Go to his site mysalsacongress.com for more information.

## AMERICAN BALLROOM

Arthur Murray Dance Studios is your best place to start if you want to explore ballroom dance. They have locations across the United States and internationally and their website is filled with great dance information. Here is their website: arthurmurray.com.

Please visit my website jamierosestudio.com, on which I will provide a more complete list of resources that I will constantly be updating. And please leave comments there! I can't wait to hear about your adventures tripping the light fantastic.

# Acknowledgments

The temptation here is to thank every person in my life who's ever been nice to me, but for the sake of brevity, I will attempt to limit myself to those who have directly helped take this book from idea to reality.

I am truly blessed to have an amazing group of friends, both new and old, who are a constant source of love and support:

Rhonda Talbot, thank you for loving me through my many incarnations, and for bringing me to Jim Krusoe's writing class. And Jim, thanks for your guidance; you taught me much about writing and about what it is to be a great teacher.

Mark Vega, thanks for cheering me on in the early stages.

Thank you to Lee Garlington for providing refuge, both literally and figuratively, and for listening to me read my entire book—laughing and crying in all the right places.

To the beautiful and talented Delauné Michel for blazing the trail, and to Joan Sittenfield, Sydney Curtis, and Martha Frankel, thank you all for being so darn fabulous.

To Michael Lally, thanks for always believing in me and in my writing and for listening patiently to all my deadline panics and fears and telling me that the fact that I was so freaked out meant I was a real writer. And thank you for spending those seventy-two grueling Skype hours going over every word of my final manuscript with me with your keen copy editor's eye and your poet's sensitive heart.

Samantha Dunn, you pushed me to get this idea on the page and believed in it from the very beginning. Your feedback and editing talents and constant reassurance that my idea could be a book made the difference between doing it and not doing it. And the doing of it has been one of the greatest joys of my life. Yes, you were right, you were right, you were right.

Thank you to Jamie Lynn Coker for introducing me to my extraordinary agent, Lynn Johnston, who then placed me under the loving guidance of editor Sara Carder and everyone at Tarcher (especially Brianna Yamashita and Andrew Yackira, aka Green-y). I don't know how I got so lucky to end up with this team.

Thank you to the wonderful Tyson Cornell and Rare Bird Lit for guiding the public journey of this book.

To my managers at Marshak/Zachary, Alan, Susan, and Darryl: thank you for sticking with me through thick and thin.

To Moti Buchboot, Lisa Pettett, Pablo Rojas, Barbara Thomas, Sergei Tumas, and Alexis White, thank you for introducing me to the dance that has changed my life in ways I never could have imagined.

To the dance teachers and performers I've had the good fortune to work with at festivals and in workshops—there are too many to list individually here, but especially Melina Brufman, Dana Frígoli, Claudio Gonzalez, Silvina Valz, Pablo Villarraza, and the late Carlos Gavito. Thank you for your glorious examples.

To the entire Los Angeles tango community, especially the promoters like Silvia Askenazi, Makela Brizuela, Yvonne Caan, Eric Dandridge, Angel Echeverria, Michael Espinoza, Stefan Fabry, Julie Friedgen, Ilona Gilarsky, Naomi Hotta, Miriam Larici, Lynn Lewin, Dimitri Lubinsky, Roberto Luque, Ruta Maria, Mitra Martin, Schwee Miguel, Laura Mingo, Monica Orozco, Emily Ortiz, Marcos Questas, Yolanda Rossi, Elizabeth Tambasco, Edmundo Thomas, and Linda Valentino: thank you for working tirelessly to bring in spectacular teachers from around the world and for making our beautiful milongas.

To my brothers and sisters of the dance, thank you for all the conversations that led to this book. Special thanks to Karlo Abouroumieh, Aliyah, Donna Amato, Claire Bainbach, Julio Ballatorre, Nancy Bleir, Monica Borunda, Laura Canellias, Trish Connery, Brenda Embrace, Vladimir Estrin, Becca Fabian, Leah Flores, Jaimes Friedgen, Madeline Gilinsky, Victor Gilinsky, Naomi Hotta, Gabriel Kaplan, Shoshana Martinez, Nikki Nash, Luiza Paes, Das Silverman, Carolyn Stewart, Mila Vigdorova, Brenda Wachel, Shannon Wilcox, Veronica Zarate, and the late Mark Celaya.

A special thank you to Lee and Chuck for the joke and to Bob Romanus for you know what.

For last-minute professional expertise, thank you to Dr. Nicki Monti; Kevin Kelly, LMFT; and Dr. Philip Stutz.

Steven Pressfield, thank you for writing *The War of Art*.

To my family, my brother Stephen; my sister-in-law Meli; my nephews Brendan, Justin, and Ethan; my step-daughter Morgan (aka Cinderella); my parents, Reta and Stewart: thank you for your steadfast love.

And, as always, thank you to my handsome, witty, talented, and loving husband, Kip Gilman: you make everything fun.

And, oh heck, I can't resist, thanks to everyone who's ever been nice to me.